Cooking in San Germán, Puerto Rico

Original cover art by Dr. Paul Vivoni Alcaráz, InterAmerican University of Puerto Rico at San Germán, Puerto Rico

Cooking in San Germán Puerto Rico

Puerto Rican Regional Cuisine

Marina Martínez de Irizarry

and

Yuyú Alcaráz vda. de Vivoni

Interior illustrations & quotes by Y.A.V.
Front cover by Dr. Paul Vivoni
New edition cover by Digna Irizarry Cassens
Front cover illustration by Manuel Torres Kortright
English Translation by Marina Martínez de Irizarry

Printed in the United Sates of America
2019 CASSENS ASSOCIATES
California

Second Edition, February 2019
Copyright 2019

This recipe book is a collection of recipes tried and tested by the original authors.
All rights reserved including the right of reproduction in whole, in any part or form.

Original copyright © 1991 by Marina Martínez de Irizarry
and
Yuyú Alcaráz vda. de Vivoni.

Original ISBN: 0-533-09278-7
Library of Congress Catalog Card No.: 90-90350

Second Edition Published by: Cassens Associates
Diversified Nutrition Management Systems
558 Tahoe Avenue, Yucca Valley, California 92284
cassensdigna@gmail.com

Second edition copyright © 2019 Cassens Associates

ISBN: 978-0-9981430-1-9

Printed and manufactured in the United States of America
First Printing 2019 Cassens Associates

Table of Contents

Topic	*Page*
Cooking in San Germán, Puerto Rico *Original Cover Illustration*	*i*
Title Page & Credits	*iii*
First Edition Copyright & Credits	*iv*
Table Of Contents	*v*
Preface	*vii*
About the Authors	*ix*
Dedication	*xi*
A Very Short History of San Germán	*xii*
Introduction	*xiii*
Glossary	*xv*
About this Book	*xvii*
Short Title Page	*xix*

Recipe Category	**Page**
Beverages and Soft Drinks	21
Appetizers	27
Soups and Stews	37
Salads	45
Egg Dishes	53
Meats	59
Poultry	75
Fish and Seafood	81
Vegetables	89
Pastas	97
Sauces	105
Fritters	111
Rice and Grains	117
Breads	127
Desserts and Candies	135
Cookies, Cakes, Icings	155
Lagniappe (Something Extra)	173
Index	179

Every meal shared with love is a big feast!

Preface

Cooking in San Germán is a compilation of regional Puerto Rican recipes from some of the best cooks in San Germán. All the recipes included were tested by Marina Martínez de Irizarry, my mother, and Yuyú Alcaráz vda. de Vivoni, her good friend and co-author. The Spanish edition (1989) and the English (1990) have been out of print since 2012. I hope you enjoy this second edition and find the recipes so delightful you'll cook them often.

This second edition is as true to the original as possible and the recipes are the same as originally written. Keeping every part of this book as authentic as possible and as part of our family heritage is my primary goal. However, some changes were necessary to meet technical requirements and different from the previous editions.

The front cover is a rendition of my favorite watercolor of the Irizarry Sambolín home where I grew up. It was portrayed by Manuel Torres Kortright, my niece's husband, in 1997. The back cover is a snapshot I took while watching my mother cook in our cheerful kitchen. Looking at this photo it's easy to imagine myself there waiting for lunch and smelling the aroma of her delicious. Most of the recipes were tested in this kitchen and served to the family. Additionally for those not familiar with the authors, Puerto Rico and San Germán I also include a few relevant photographs in the introduction section.

The first page of the interior is the original books cover for the first cditions and is an illustration by Dr. Paul Vivoni Alcaráz, Yuyú's son. The unique interior illustrations and quotes are Yuyú's original design. She was a talented and versatile artist. Credit for typing the original manuscript, communicating with the publishers and marketing goes to my father, Milton Irizarry Sambolín. He also did all the driving to classes and demonstrations and did the heavy lifting; carrying groceries and some of the advance preparation. Of course, his favorite job was tasting the recipes with gusto.

My mother inspired me to respect and love food, create delicious food and write about it. Comfort food was her specialty and she was known for her hospitality. I've enjoyed a long career in nutrition as a registered dietitian nutritionist and have published 9 books prior to this one, 3 of them cookbooks. It has been a sweet memory, a pleasure and a privilege for me to work on this edition.

Digna Irizarry Cassens, MHA, RDN, CLT, FAND

About the Authors

MARINA MARTÍNEZ de IRIZARRY, was a Home Economics graduate from the University of Radford, she worked I the Schoolroom Lunch Program and in the Home Economics Program of InterAmerican University. Married for 50 years to Mr. Milton Irizarry Sambolín, father of her two children, Digna Marina, Dietitian, and Dr. Milton Irizarry, Dentist. Marina is the kind of woman that chooses a path and follows it without looking at the obstacles in he way. Her love and devotion for all her family, strength of character, her realism and sincerity, help her to defy life with a smile. And Marina is a great-grandmother.

Died in California in 2014 where she lived with her daughter during her last years

YUYÚ ALCARÁZ VDA. de VIVONI graduated B.A. from Polytechnic Institute, known today as InterAmerican University. Her marriage to Mr. Pedro Pascual Vivoni ended upon his death in 1982. Mother of three sons, Pedro Juan, Tomás *(deceased)*, Paul, and a very "special" daughter, Maríanne *(deceased)*. Yuyú's devotion to her children was acknowledged when she was selected San Germán's Mother of the Year in 1985. Yuyú has had the strength to withstand the hardships and she has enjoyed all the good things she has been blessed with. Her family, her God and her friends are her priorities and her solace.

Died in San Germán, Puerto Rico in 2017 in her family home

Dedication
1986

While writing the dedication for this book, thoughts of my childhood home kept coming to my mind……my kind mother whom I lost at a very young age……my father and my aunt. I also remember my mother-in-law who was like a mother to me, and her husband, because together with them, my husband Milton and our two children, lived in a house filled with love. I cannot omit mentioning Maríanne, because through her I have learned to see life with more tolerance and love.

Marina Martínez de Irizarry

I dedicate this book to the memory of my dear- parents, to my unforgettable husband, Pedro Pascual, and to my four children Pedro Juan, Tomás, Paul and Maríanne, because they have given meaning to my life.

Yuyú Alcaráz vda. de Vivoni

A Very Short History of San Germán

One of the oldest towns in the Americas, San Germán was originally founded in 1512. Due to Indian as well as English and French pirate attacks, the town was moved to several locations until the year 1570 when it was finally settled in the Hills of Santa Marta, its present site. For this reason it is also known as the City of Hills (la Ciudad de las Lomas).

It is a lovely town with beautiful Victorian houses and old buildings, rich in traditions and with a colorful heritage. Its people are known for their warmth and friendliness.

San Germán boasts the oldest church of the Americas, Porta Coeli, built in 1528. It is a museum today.

Introduction

Marina Martínez de Irizarry, Yuyú Alcaráz vda. de Vivoni

It was not our purpose to write another cookbook. Our desire was been to compile the recipes that we inherited from our mothers, from our grandmothers, from our neighbors and friends; recipes that we asked for in our wish to serve to our families a varied menu, and that in some way would give continuity to our lives. We have added recipes given to us by friends who came from other countries, but that now feel *Sangermeñas*.

To all we simply say THANK YOU...with all the emotion that we feel as we remember our loved ones, many already gone from our lives, but always present in our memories… They, by their example, inspired in us the desire to be better wives, better mothers and better housewives. For them, Oh Lord, we ask Your blessings.

The Iglesia San Germán de Auxerre *is a historic Roman Catholic parish church located in San Germán, Puerto Rico, overlooking the main plaza. Spanish settlers founded San Germán parish in 1510 and built the first permanent church in 1688. Daily services are still held in this church.*

Glossary

ANNATO OIL. Use for coloring food. Boil ¼ cup annato seeds in ¾ cup vegetable oil. Strain and keep refrigerated.

CHORIZO. Spanish sausage. Canned or dry.

CILANTRO. *Cilantrillo* or Chinese parsley. Fresh leaves are used. The seeds are called coriander.

COCONUT MILK. Made from the meat of the dry coconuts. Canned coconut milk is available in Spanish markets, sweetened as well as unsweetened.

CULANTRO. Long leaves about 3 to 5 inches long and serrated edges. Strong smell.

GUAVA PASTE. Available in Spanish markets.

HOLLAND BALL CHEESE. Very similar to Edam cheese but has a harder shell. To make stuffed cheese Holland cheese is preferred because of the hard shell.

SAZÓN or SASÓN. Special Spanish seasoning sold in Spanish markets and other grocery stores. It is a mixture of seasonings.

SOFRITO. You can make your own sofrito (see index). If the ingredients listed are not available use only the ones you can find. You may add onions.

SWEET CHILES. Not hot. Light bell pepper flavor.

OFFAL. The main ingredient of **Gandinga** consisting of the organs inside an animal, such as the brain, the heart, and the liver, eaten as food. Gandinga is a word of African roots used in Puerto Rico to describe a stew made with organ beef or pork meats. Recipe in page 63.

About this Book

Original publication with the ISBN: 0-533-09278-7. Vantage Press, Inc. New York, New York

Cooking in San Germán, Puerto Rico: *Puerto Rican Regional Cuisine*, by Marina Martínez de Irizarry and Yuyú Alcaráz vda. de Vivoni, is chock-full of delectable recipes and will add a wealth of variety to the menus of any family. From Spiced Brew to Butter Icing, each page has recipes that will stir the creative cook's imagination. Although most of the recipes are fine examples of Puerto Rican cuisine, these cooks of San Germán also borrowed from other lands, and these recipes are included as well. This book covers beverages and soft drinks, appetizers, soups and stews, salads, egg dishes, meats, poultry, fish and seafood, vegetables, pastas, sauces, fritters, rice and grains, breads, desserts and candies, and cookies cakes and icings. There are labor-intensive recipes and quick ones, but all are guaranteed to produce scrumptious results. The charming illustrations by Ms. Vda.de Vivoni combine with the mouth-watering recipes to make this book a joy, for novice and experienced cooks alike. Read, cook, and enjoy.

Quote from the first edition original back cover

Cooking in San Germán Puerto Rico

Beverages and Soft Drinks

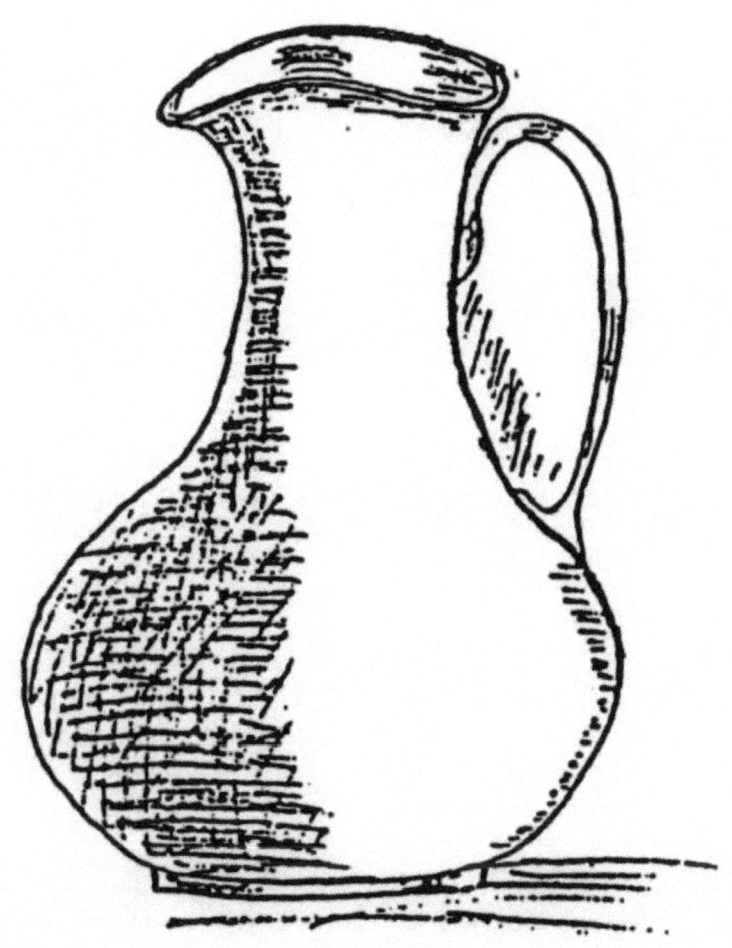

Hospitality is a token of fraternal love.....

SPICED BREW
(Refresco de Especias (Agua Loja)

1 piece fresh ginger	4 cups water
4 sticks cinnamon	1 cup molasses

Wash and then pound with a mallet the fresh ginger. Boil for 10 minutes together with the cinnamon. Cool, strain, add molasses. For a sweeter brew add more molasses to taste. Serve cold.

EGG NOG "PAPAI"
(Ponche "Papai")

5 cups sugar	3 (12 oz. cans) evaporated milk
2 cups water	1 quart rum
8 egg yolks	1 – 3 sticks cinnamon

Boil water, sugar and cinnamon to make a heavy syrup. Remove from stove and carefully add the rum while syrup is still warm. Stir for a while and let cool. Beat egg yolks until lemon colored, add evaporated milk mixing well. Add to the other mixture. Pass through a strainer and pour into clean bottles. Refrigerate.
Makes 3 1/2 quarts. Keeps well in refrigerator for years.

KAHLUA "THE SPIDERS"
(Kahlúa Las Arañitas)

2 1/2 cups water	5 tablespoons instant coffee granules
3 3/4 cups sugar	2 tablespoons glycerin
2 teaspoons vanilla	$4/5^{th}$ bottle Vodka

Boil sugar and 2 cups water for about 40 minutes (240' F.) Remove from stove, add vanilla. With the 1/2 cup water you reserved, dissolve coffee granules and add to the syrup. Add glycerin and let cool. Add Vodka and beat well. Pour into bottles. Refrigerate. Makes two $4/5^{th}$ bottles.

ISLAND COCONUT EGG NOG
(Coquito Isleño)

8 egg yolks	1 teaspoon ground cinnamon
1 cup sugar	1 (12 oz. can) evaporated milk
2 teaspoons vanilla	1
1 quart rum	1 15 oz. cans) sweetened coconut milk

Beat egg yolks, sugar and vanilla until creamy. Add nutmeg, cinnamon, evaporated milk, coconut milk and rum slowly and stir until well mixed. Strain, pour into bottles and refrigerate. Keeps well in the refrigerator.

DELICIOUS HOT CHOCOLATE
(Chocolate Caliente Sabroso)

2 cups water	1 oz. unsweetened chocolate
1/2 lb. sweet chocolate	1 quart milk

Melt chocolate in hot water at very low temperature, stirring and scraping the bottom of the pan to keep the chocolate from sticking. When completely dissolved add milk and cook at low temperature, stirring constantly.
Each time it boils up, move away from heat and stir.
Do this three times. Remove from stove and beat with a ladle until it foams up.

IRISH CREAM "NENAI"
(Crema Irlandesa "Nenai")

1 1/3 cups liquor (Rum, Whiskey or Brandy)	2 tablespoons chocolate syrup
1 (14 oz.) can condensed milk	2 teaspoons instant coffee
1 cup light cream- half and half	1 teaspoon vanilla
4 eggs	½ teaspoon almond extract

Mix all ingredients together by hand or in blender. Strain and pour into bottles. Refrigerate. Keeps well.

COFFEE EGG NOG "LÍA"
(Ponche de Café "Lía")

1 quart milk	4 teaspoons instant coffee
4 egg yolks	1 cup liquor (Brandy or Rum)
1 cup + 4 tablespoons sugar	2 sticks cinnamon

Beat egg yolks with the 4 tablespoons sugar. Heat milk with 1 cup sugar and cinnamon sticks. Remove from heat.
Add the beaten egg yolks and cook this mixture at low temperature stirring all the time until it starts to thicken (15 to 20 minutes). Remove from stove, add instant coffee slowly and beat until all the granules are dissolved. Add liquor, stir, strain and pour into bottles. Refrigerate.

SANTA ROSA SANGRÍA
(Sangria "Santa Rosa")

2 or 3 green limes	1 apple
2 oranges	1 bottle red wine
1 cup sugar	1 (12 oz.) bottle Soda water

Slice one lime and one orange--remove seeds. Place in a glass pitcher with 1 cup sugar and stir well with wooden spoon. Dice unpeeled apple and add to the pitcher stirring well. Add juice of the other orange and juice of 1 or 2 limes. Add the wine, taste and add more sugar if needed. Let sit in refrigerator. When ready to serve add ice cubes, stir to chill, then add Soda water and serve immediately.

SPIKED ICED TEA
(Refresco de Té)

2 cups strong tea
1 cup grape juice
1 cups orange juice
1/4 cup lime juice
1 cup sugar
1/2 cup water
1 cans beer

Boil water with sugar to make a syrup. In a pitcher mix all juices and tea. Sweeten adding sugar syrup to taste. When ready to serve add ice cubes and beer. Serve chilled.

PARTY PUNCH
(Ponche para Fiestas)

4 cups guava juice
6 cups orange juice
4 cups pineapple juice
1/2 cup lime juice

4 cups sugar
3 cans beer
3 cans Soda (Ginger Ale or 7Up

Mix all juices and sugar. When ready to serve add ice, then Soda and beer. You can also add canned fruit cocktail. (Optional)

Appetizers

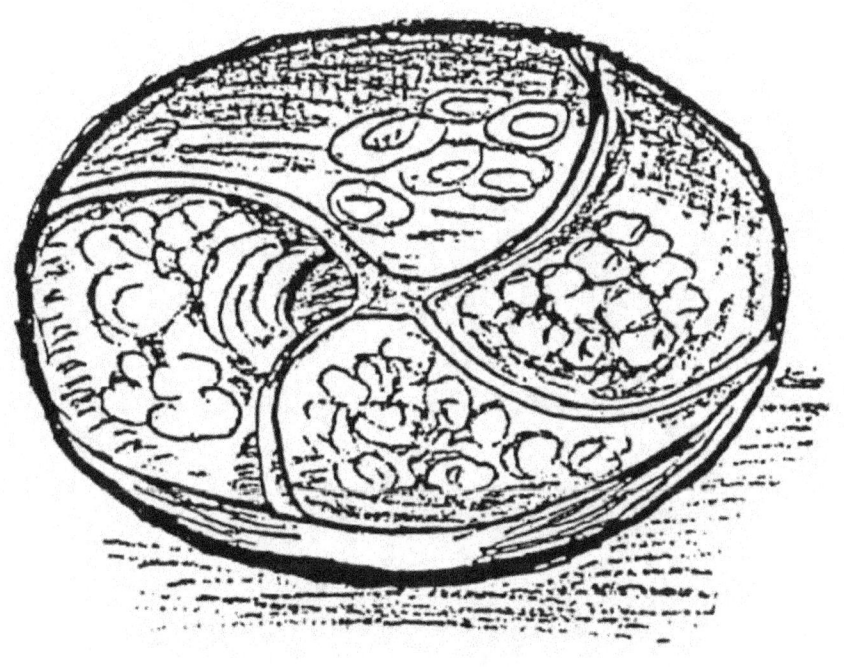

Let us thank God for small things.....

ANTIPASTO "MAMÉ"

(Antipasto "Mamé")

2 medium eggplants	1/2 cup catsup
3 tablespoons olive oil	1 can tuna fish
2 or 3 carrots-sliced	salt to taste
1 medium onion	black pepper
1 tablespoon vinegar	1 (8 oz) can tomato sauce
1/2 cup stuffed olives-sliced	1 small can sliced
3 or 4 sour pickles-sliced	mushrooms

Peel eggplants and cut in 4 pieces. Boil in small amount of water until soft but still whole. Remove skins and seeds and chop. Heat olive oil, add sliced carrots and cook at very low temperature. Slice onion by first cutting in half, then set the cut side on a chopping block and slice with a downward movement of the knife. Cook together with the carrots at very low temperature until the carrots are cooked. Add eggplant, vinegar, tomato sauce, mushrooms, olives, pickles, tuna fish and mix well. You can also add artichokes. Refrigerate. Keeps well.

ANTIPASTO "PEPEVÉ"
(Antipasto "Pepevé")

1 lb. chicken breasts	1 bottle catsup
1 teaspoon salt	1/2 cup vinegar
2 medium onions	10 black peppercorns
2 garlic cloves	or 1 teaspoon ground pepper
1/2 cup olive oil	1 jalapeño pepper (optional)
2 cups shredded cabbage	

Boil chicken with salt, garlic and 1 whole onion until tender. Chop 1 onion and sauté in olive oil with shredded cabbage for 15 to 20 minutes. Be careful it does not brown. With fingers, shred chicken meat discarding skin and bones. Add chicken to pan, add vinegar, catsup and sliced jalapeño pepper. Mix well, cool and refrigerate. Serve with soda crackers or saltines. Keeps well in refrigerator.

MY MOTHER'S COCKTAIL ONIONS
(Cebollitas de Mi Madre)

1 lb. small onions
2 slices bacon
1 teaspoon salt
1/2 cup dry wine

Cook bacon on low temperature until it renders all fat. Remove bacon, sauté onions in the bacon fat, at very low temperature. Do not let onions brown. Add salt and wine and cook for 20 minutes until golden in color. Serve as appetizer or with meats.

RAINBOW SANDWICH
(Arco Iris de Pan)

1 loaf sandwich bread-sliced lengthwise

Spread one side of each slice with butter. Spread one slice with tuna filling, buttered side up, a second slice with egg salad filling, and a third slice with Deviled Ham filling. Place one on top of the other. Place the last slice of bread, buttered side DOWN over the last slice. Press down with hands, then wrap tightly in a wet, clean kitchen towel. Refrigerate. Soften cream cheese with milk and spread all over the sandwich stack--top and sides. Refrigerate. Decorate with sliced stuffed olives, pimiento slices, asparagus. Cut in slices.

TUNA SALAD FILLING - Mix 1 can tuna fish , mayonnaise, grated onion, chopped green peppers and black pepper.

EGG SALAD FILLING - Mash 4 hard boiled eggs, add 3 tablespoons mayonnaise, 1 teaspoon vinegar, 1 tablespoon grated onion, 1/2 teaspoon ground curry, salt and pepper.

DEVILED HAM FILLING - Mix 1 can Deviled Ham, 1 tablespoon mayonnaise, 1 chopped canned pimiento and 1 chopped sweet pickle. Add red food coloring (optional).

TURKEY ROLL
(Embutido de Pavo)

1 1/2 lbs. turkey breast
1/4 lb. chicken livers
1 tablespoon margarine
1/2 lb. boiled ham
5 eggs
1 cup cracker meal

2 teaspoons grated onion
3/4 teaspoon salt
1/4 teaspoon nutmeg
1/4 teaspoon black pepper
2 tablespoons Paprika

Sauté chicken livers in margarine, grind together with turkey breast and boiled ham. Beat 3 eggs until foamy, add to the meats with 3 tablespoons cracker meal, onion, salt, nutmeg and black pepper mixing well. Divide In two portions and place on two separate pieces of wax paper, forming two rolls about 10 inches long. Roll in cracker- meal. Beat 2 eggs, dip rolls in the eggs, again roll in cracker meal. Have ready two pieces of clean fabric about 16 inches square- old napkins will do fine- to wrap the rolls tightly. Tie with cord. Have ready enough boiling salted water to cover rolls. Drop rolls in boiling water, let water return to boiling. Boil for 1 hour, turning once. Remove rolls from water and let cool. Peel off cloth and wrap rolls in Saran wrap or wax paper. Refrigerate. When ready to serve, roll in Paprika. Slice very thin.

OLD TIMES FOIE GRAS
(Foie Gras de Aquí)

½ lb. chicken livers
¼ cup softened butter
1 hard boiled egg
1/2 lb. boiled ham
1/3 lb. Holland or Edam cheese

1 small onion
½ lb. cured ham
1 can pimentos (2 ½ oz)
½ teaspoon salt

Boil livers in 2 cups water with salt and onion until water boils down to 1 cup. Grind pimientos, drained boiled livers, cheese, boiled egg yolk and softened butter, adding some of the water livers were boiled in, stirring to make a soft paste. Black pepper may be added to taste.
Refrigerate.

PATE "MAMÉ"
(Paté "Mamé")

1 lb. ground chicken livers	4 or 5 eggs
1/2 lb. ground pork	1 1/2 teaspoons salt
1/8 teaspoon ground cloves	1/2 teaspoon black pepper
2 bay leaves	1/4 lb. lard- to grease the mold
1 sprig parsley	

Mix chicken livers, pork, salt, black pepper, bay leaves and parsley. Cover and refrigerate overnight. Next day remove bay leaves, add ground cloves and beaten eggs, mixing well. Grease mold with the lard. Put the mixture in the pan, press down, cover with aluminum foil. Place pan on unit on top of the stove turned on high until the meat starts to sizzle, then place in 350' F oven for 1 1/2 hours. Insert a tooth pick or cake tester to test for doneness. Take out of the oven, let cool some, but while still warm take the grease the meat juices. Take out mash with a fork and place get rid of air bubbles, film on top so it will out being careful not to empty the meat juices. Take out of the mold while still warm, mash with a fork and place in a paté mold pressing hard to get rid of air bubbles. Pour some of the grease in a thin film on top so it will keep better. Refrigerate.

ONION QUICHE
(Quiche de Cebollas)

1 pie crust- uncooked	4 eggs
4 slices bacon- fried and crumbled	1 cup milk
1 large onion- diced	2 cups Holland or Edam cheese
1/4 cup margarine	1 tsp garlic salt
2 tablespoons flour	1/8 tsp black pepper

Sauté onion in rendered bacon fat, add flour and mix. Beat eggs, mix in milk, salt and pepper. Add to the other- ingredients. Pour into pie shell. Bake in 400'F oven for 15 minutes, turn temperature down to 350' F for 20 to 25 minutes. Serve warm.

GIZZARDS "MAMÁ INA"
(Mollejas "Mamá Ina")

1 lb. chicken gizzards	1 large onion- chopped
1/4 lb. butter	1/2 cup stuffed olives-chopped
1 teaspoon salt	1 small can pimiento-chopped
1/4 teaspoon black pepper	1/2 cup red wine

Clean gizzards, wash and cut in pieces. Cook in a heavy pot with butter and onions on low heat for 3 hours or until tender, stirring often. Add olives, pimiento and wine. Cook for 5 minutes at low temperature. Serve cold.

LATIN PATE
(Paté Latino)

3 (6 ¾ oz.) cans Hormel Chunky Chicken (or any canned chicken)
3 (5 oz.) cans Spam Deviled Luncheon Meat — Worcestershire sauce
3 envelopes unflavored gelatin — ½ teaspoon nutmeg
1/3 cup water — 1 teaspoon salt

Dissolve gelatin in water. Beat all ingredients together in electric mixer, slowly at the beginning, then faster. Mix in dissolved gelatin. Pour in mold and refrigerate. You can cover with a spread made with cream cheese, grated onion and mayonnaise beaten together. Refrigerate.

TUNA MOUSSE
(Molde de Atún)

1 can Cream of Asparagus soup	½ cup hot water
1 (3 oz.) cream cheese	1 (3 oz.) cream cheese
2 envelopes unflavored gelatin	2 envelopes unflavored gelatin

Heat Cream of Asparagus soup with the cream cheese at very low temperature. Dissolve gelatin in hot water. Mix all ingredients together and pour in mold. Refrigerate until the next day. To unmold set the pan in hot water for 1 minute.

CHICKEN LIVERS MOUSSE
(Mousse de Hígado de Pollo)

1 lb. chicken livers
2 tablespoons butter
2 tablespoons chopped onions
1 teaspoon salt
1/8 teaspoon black pepper

1/4 teaspoon thyme
3/4 cups butter-softened
2 tablespoons Brandy
1/2 cup whipped cream

Sauté livers in 2 tablespoons butter. for 5 minutes. Add chopped onions and cook for 5 minutes. Add salt, pepper, thyme, softened butter and Brandy. Whip in the blender or put through a sieve. Fold in whipped cream. Refrigerate.

BORÍNQUEN PATE
(Paté Criollo)

2 tablespoons olive oil
1 can sliced mushrooms
1 onion- chopped
1 garlic clove- chopped
1/4 cup Sherry wine
1 teaspoon salt
1/2 teaspoon thyme
1/2 teaspoon black

1/8 teaspoon nutmeg
1/2 lb. ground pork
1/2 chicken breast
1 egg -beaten
1/3 cup parsley- chopped
1/2 lb. bacon
1/4 cup pistachios

Sauté garlic, onion and mushrooms in olive oil. Add wine, salt, pepper, thyme and nutmeg. Simmer for 3 minutes. Cool, Mix with the ground meats, pistachios, egg 3nd 2 tablespoons chopped parsley. Line a loaf pan (8"x4") with bacon, laying the bacon strips across the narrow side of the mold, with the ends hanging over the sides. Sprinkle parsley, then spoon the meat mixture, pressing down to remove air pockets Fold bacon strips over meat. Press to seal. Bake in 350' F oven for 1 1/4 hours. Cut a piece of cardboard to fit the mold and wrap it in aluminum foil . Place over the meat, weight with a heavy skillet. Refrigerate overnight.
To unmold dip in hot water for 1 minute.

MARINATED MUSHROOMS
(Setas Marinada)

1 small onion- chopped	1/4 teaspoon black pepper
3 tablespoons olive oil	2 tablespoons Brandy
2 (6 oz .) cans whole mushrooms	juice of 1 lime
1/4 teaspoon salt	

Sauté onion in olive oil. Add drained mushrooms and sauté for several minutes. Add salt, pepper, Brandy and lime juice. Turn off heat and let sit for a while.

LITTLE DEVILS
(Diablotines)

1 loaf French bread	salt
4 egg yolks	Paprika
1 cup Parmesan cheese	

Slice bread thinly, spread slices with a mixture of beaten egg yolks, Parmesan cheese and salt. Set on baking sheet and bake in 425' F oven for 8 to 10 minutes. Remove from oven and dust with Paprika.

CARIBBEAN CAVIAR
(Caviar Criollo)

2 medium sized eggplants	1/4 cup vinegar
1/2 cup chopped onions	1 bay leaf
1 teaspoon chopped garlic	salt
3/4 cup olive oil	black pepper

Peel eggplants, dice and boil salt a cup of water with salt and 1 tablespoon vinegar. Sauté onions in olive oil with bay leaf, garlic, vinegar and black pepper. Drain eggplant and add to the sautéed mixture, stirring until well mixed and mushy.

Refrigerate. Serve cold with crackers.

Soups and Stews

Think......
And then act.....

GARLIC SOUP

(Sopa de Ajo)

3 tablespoons olive oil
6 garlic cloves-chopped
6 cups water

3 cubes chicken consommé
4 eggs

Sauté garlic in oil. Remove pan from heat, add water and consommé cubes. Return to heat and simmer for 2 minutes. While consommé simmers, beat eggs with a fork, only to mix yolks and whites. Drop beaten eggs in a thin stream into the boiling consommé. This can be easily done with the help of a fork. Let consommé come to a boil again until the eggs cook. You can also drop unbeaten eggs, one at a time into the boiling consommé and let simmer until cooked.

CODFISH ASOPAO
(Asopao de Bacalao)

1/2 lb. salt codfish
1 cup fresh sofrito
2 tablespoons tomato sauce

2 tablespoons olive oil
6 cups water
2 cups rice

Cut salt codfish in large pieces. Soak overnight or boil once until it flakes. Discard bones and skin. Flake codfish. Make sofrito and cook in olive oil over low heat. Add tomato sauce and codfish and cook for 5 minutes more. Add rice, correct salt and boil until rice is cooked. You may add olives and capers. Serve with side dishes of pimientos, asparagus and green peas. For sofrito, see Index.

BOLLITOS
(Small Buns)

6 green bananas
garlic salt

Grate green bananas or process in food processor with garlic salt. Drop from a tablespoon into boiling soup and simmer until cooked. Delicious in any soup.

GARLIC AND ONION SOUP
(Sopa de Cebolla y Ajo)

6 garlic cloves-chopped
2 cups onions-thinly sliced
1 cup green and red peppers-chopped
3 tablespoons olive oil
2 cups fresh tomatoes-chopped

4 cups chicken consommé or broth
3 slices sandwich bread – crust removed
French bread sliced, toasted
Parmesan Cheese to taste

Sauté onions, garlic, green and red peppers, in olive oil for about 15 minutes. Add consommé and tomatoes. Simmer for 10 minutes. Add sandwich bread broken in small pieces, and boil to thicken soup. Add salt and black pepper to taste. Place one slice of toasted French bread in a plate and ladle soup over bread. Sprinkle with Parmesan cheese.

GALICIAN SOUP
(Caldo Gallego)

1/2 lb. stewing chicken pieces
1/2 lb. pork meat- cut up
1/4 lb. ham- cut up
2 large potatoes
2 or 3 carrots
1 bay leaf
6 cups water

1 lb. navy beans
2 chorizos
1 piece (½) cabbage
onion
garlic
green peppers
1 teaspoon salt

Soak beans overnight. Make a good soup stock with the meats. Add beans and the other ingredients. Simmer for about 2 hours. Correct salt. You may also add water watercress, canned or fresh string beans or spinach.

PIGEON PEA *(GANDULES)* STEW
(Sopón de Gandules)

1 lb. pigeon peas (gandules)	2 tablespoons tomato sauce
1/2 lb. pork meat	1 lb. yautía or potatoes- diced
6 cups water	fresh cilantro
1 green pepper -chopped	long leaf cilantro
1 onion- chopped	orégano
2 garlic cloves	salt
1 tomato- chopped	1/4 cup rice

Boil pork and pigeon peas in 6 cups salted water. Sauté green pepper, onion, garlic, tomato, fresh cilantro, long leaf culantro, orégano and tomato sauce. Add to pigeon peas and boil for 15 minutes. Add yautía or potatoes and rice. Simmer, add "bollitos" and let simmer until cooked. This is a thick soup. For a thinner soup add water or broth.

GARBANZO PURÉE
(Puré de Garbanzos)

1 beef or chicken pieces	1 carrot
1 onion	1 can garbanzo beans
1 green pepper	4 cups water
1 tomato	1 tablespoon olive oil
1 sprig cilantro	salt

Boil meat, onion, green pepper, tomato, cilantro and carrots to make a good broth. Add garbanzos and let boil. Remove the meat, sieve the soup or process in blender. Return soup and meat to pot, add salt and olive oil. Heat and serve, topped with chopped parsley and garlic bread or croutons.

GARBANZO SOUP WITH CHICKEN
(Sopa de Garbanzos con Pollo)

1 cup dry garbanzo beans or 1 can boiled garbanzos
4 chicken pieces

4 cups chicken consommé	1 onion- chopped
4 garlic cloves	1/4 teaspoon cumin
1 bay leaf	1 tablespoon .lime juice
1 cinnamon stick	2 tablespoons parsley
2 whole cloves	2 tablespoons olive oil

Soak garbanzos overnight. Boil garbanzos in chicken -consommé. Add chicken pieces, garlic, onion, bay leaf, cinnamon and cloves. Boil for 45 minutes. If using canned garbanzos boil only 20 minutes. Remove meat and about 1 cup garbanzos to another pot. Pure in blender the other mixture or pass through a strainer. Add to the meat and garbanzos in the other pot. Sauté onion in olive oil and add to soup. Add cumin and simmer for 10 minutes. Add lime juice and chopped parsley. Let rest to blend flavors.

CHILI
(Sopa de Habichuelas ó Chile)

4 cans red kidney beans	2 tablespoons sugar
2 lbs. ground beef	1 cup catsup
1 onion- chopped	ground chili to taste
2 cans whole tomatoes	salt to taste
5 cans water	

Simmer all ingredients together for 1 hour stirring often. Add ground chili and salt to taste. Let sit to blend flavors.

"MOFONGO" AND EGG SOUP
(Sopa de Mofongo con Huevos)

Make a good stock with:
1 lb. beef and 1/2 lb. beef for about in 2 quarts water. Simmer for about 1/2 hour.
Add:

1 tablespoon salt	fresh cilantro leaves
1 onion	1 green pepper
2 garlic cloves	2 sweet chiles
1 tomato	Eggs (1 per person)

Simmer for 2 hours.

"MOFONGO":

3 green plantains
3 garlic cloves
Salt to taste

Peel plantains, cut into pieces and soak in salted water . Fry plantains in deep fat. Mash with garlic while still hot. Add "Mofongo" to simmering broth . Drop eggs into broth, one at a time and simmer until eggs cook.

SOUP FOR LENT
(Sopa de Cuaresma)

1 onion- chopped	1/2 cup diced pumpkin
4 tablespoons margarine	½ cup shredded cabbage
3 tablespoons olive oil	1 tablespoon salt
1/2 cup thinly sliced carrots	½ tsp. white pepper
1/2 cup diced celery	Chopped parsley
1/2 cup diced potatoes	Chopped cilantro
6 cups water	Chopped long-leaf culantro or cumin
1/2 cup diced yautía (tanier)	

Sauté onion in margarine and olive oil. Add vegetables, a small amount at a time, stirring well. Sauté vegetables for 5 minutes. Add water and seasonings and simmer for 1/2 hour or longer, as needed. Add other vegetables for variety. read.

CATALONIAN SOUP
(Cocido a la Catalana)

several chicken pieces	4 cups water
1 lb. beef	1 lb. garbanzo beans-(soaked overnight)

Simmer for 30 minutes. Add:

1/4 lb. cooking ham	1/4 lb. salt pork
1 1/2 lbs. potatoes	2 tomatoes- chopped
1 piece cabbage	2 onions- chopped

Simmer for 30 minutes: Add:

THE CATALONIAN MEAT BALL

1/2 lb. ground pork	2 cups bread-soaked in milk
1/2 lb. ground beef	2 eggs
4 oz. ground ham	salt - pepper
2 oz. ground salt pork	ground cinnamon
chopped onion	ground nutmeg
chopped green pepper	flour
chopped parsley	

Mix all ingredients together, shape into a ball, roll in flour and drop gently in the simmering soup. Simmer for about 20 minutes. Let rest before serving to blend flavors. You may substitute canned garbanzos for dry garbanzos.

Salads

God blesses the woman who does her chores with love....

MACARONI AND SHRIMP SALAD
(Ensalada de Coditos con Camarones)

1 cup boiled elbow macaroni
5 hard boiled eggs- chopped
2 cans pimientos- chopped
1/2 cup stuffed olives- sliced
1/2 cup pickled onions
1/2 cup sweet pickles- chopped

½ cup mayonnaise
Salt
Black pepper
Vinegar
1 lb. boiled shrimp (peeled & veined)

Mix all ingredients together. Refrigerate and serve on lettuce leaves.

FLORIDA SALAD
(Ensalada Florida)

4 or more carrots
4 green peppers- chopped
4 red peppers- chopped
1/2 lb. onions- sliced thin
1/2 teaspoon Worcestershire sauce

1/3 cup olive oil
1/3 cup wine vinegar
3 tablespoons mustard
Black pepper

Cut carrots in long, thin strips. Drop carrots in boiling salted water, strain immediately and cool in cold running water. Sauté the onions in olive oil and add to carrots. Add olive oil to the pan and sauté green and red peppers, only until wilted. Add peppers to the carrot/onion mixture. Mix together the mustard, olive oil, Worcestershire sauce, vinegar, salt and black pepper. Add this sauce to the vegetables, mix well and let rest in the refrigerator to blend flavors.

PEAR SALAD
(Ensalada de Peras)

2 envelopes unflavored gelatin
1/2 cup orange juice
1 (12 oz) can evaporated milk
1 can pear halves
1 (8 oz) cream cheese
1 tablespoon sugar

Mix well cream cheese, sugar, about half of the pear syrup and evaporated milk. Dissolve gelatin in cold orange juice. Heat the reserved pear syrup and add to the orange juice. Add to cream cheese mixture, mixing well. Add pears, in halves or sliced. Freeze for one hour and then move to the refrigerator. Serve over lettuce leaves, with mayonnaise or cottage cheese and other fruits if desired.

POTATO ROLL
(Rollo de Papas)

3 lbs. boiled potatoes
spiced ham (Spam, Hormel, Tulip)
hard boiled eggs
pimientos
sweet pickles
olive oil
mayonnaise
butter

While the potatoes are boiling, grind the spiced ham, pimientos, pickles, and mix well with the mayonnaise. Cut the eggs in quarters, lengthwise. Mash the potatoes with the olive oil and butter to make a smooth paste, not too soft. Cut a piece of wax paper about 14 to 16 inches long. Spread the mashed potatoes on the wax paper, forming a rectangle. Spoon the filling in a long line in the center of the mashed potatoes and place the quartered eggs over the filling. Fold wax paper over all to form a roll, tucking in paper at both ends and pressing down as you roll to get rid of air bubbles and form a compact roll. Refrigerate. Slice and serve on lettuce leaves.

CRAZY CHICKEN SALAD
(Ensalada Pollo Loco)

3 lbs. chicken breasts- boiled and cubed	1 stalk celery – cut up
1 (5 oz) can diced carrots	1 (8 oz.) can green peas - drained
1 (8 oz) jar sandwich spread	1 apple – peeled & sliced
1 (8 oz) jar mayonnaise	1 (8 oz.) cream cheese
2 lbs. boiled potatoes- diced	1 can asparagus - drained

Mix all ingredients together. Add salt & pepper to taste. Refrigerate until ready to serve.

SPRING SALAD
(Ensalada Primavera)

4 oz. pasta	1 tablespoon chopped onion
1 cup fresh broccoli	1 teaspoon lime juice
1/2 cup green peas	¼ cup evaporated milk
1 fresh red pepper- sliced	Black pepper
1 tomato- diced	

Boil pasta according to package directions, drain and rinse in cold water. Separate the broccoli in small florets. Combine pasta, broccoli florets, green peas, chopped red pepper, tomato and onion in a bowl. In a separate bowl mix evaporated milk, lime juice and black pepper and add to pasta, tossing to combine well. Refrigerate.

STUFFED TOMATOES
(Tomates Rellenos)

4 tomatoes	Mayonnaise
boiled ham- diced	Chopped onions
hard boiled eggs	salt

Cut a slice off the top of each tomato. Scoop out the pulp and reserve. Separate hard boiled eggs, yolks in one bowl and whites in another bowl. Mix yolks with mayonnaise, onions and boiled ham, m mixing well. Add reserved tomato pulp and mix gently. Season to taste. Spoon this mixture into tomatoes. Chop egg whites, spoon mayonnaise on top of filled tomatoes and garnish with chopped egg whites.

OTHER FILLINGS
Anchovies, sardines, stuffed chopped olives, hard boiled eggs, olive oil and vinegar. Add lime or lemon juice and tomato pulp.

RAINBOW SALAD "YUYA"
(Ensalada Arco Iris "Yuya")

2 lbs. potatoes- boiled	1 can pimentos (2 ½ oz.)
2 tablespoons margarine	1 can spiced ham
milk	Grated onion
1 (8 oz) can green peas	

Mash potatoes with margarine and milk to a smooth paste. In separate bowls, mash green peas, spiced ham and canned pimientos- each in its own bowl. To each bowl add chopped onions. Divide the mashed potatoes in 4 equal portions. In a well buttered mold spread a layer of mashed potatoes, a layer of green peas filling, a second layer of mashed potatoes, a layer of spiced ham, and then a fourth layer of mashed potatoes. Smooth the top with a spoon dipped in milk or melted butter. Refrigerate overnight. Unmold on a platter and slice to serve on lettuce leaves. You may line the mold with buttered wax paper to make it easier to unmold.

SALAD BOAT
(Bote de Ensalada)

1 loaf French bread	1 tablespoon chopped onions
4 hard boiled eggs	1/2 teaspoon minced garlic
1 cup chopped boiled ham	1/2 teaspoon salt
1 cup chopped celery	1/2 teaspoon mustard
2 chopped sweet pickles	2 tablespoons melted butter
12 chopped stuffed olives	

Mix together all ingredients except the butter. Cut the bread in half, lengthwise. Scoop out some of the center to make room for the filling and add this bread pulp to the other ingredients, mixing well. Fill the bottom half of bread with the filling and top with the other half, pressing down . Place the loaf of bread on a large piece of aluminum foil and brush top with melted butter. Wrap loaf in the aluminum foil and set in 350' F oven for 30 minutes, slice and serve while still warm.

MORSEL FROM THE SEA
(Ensalada Bocado del Mar)

1 lb potatoes – boiled & mashed	1 can pimentos – drained & chopped
1 can salmon -drained & mashed with fork	1 cup mayonnaise
1 large sweet pickle – chopped	1 (8 oz.) cream cheese)

Combine mashed potatoes, salmon, pickle and pimientos. Beat cream cheese and mayonnaise and add to the potato mixture. Mix well. Refrigerate, covered, to let flavors blend. Serve over lettuce leaves. Can be shaped into balls with an ice cream scoop to form a half ball. Garnish with hard boiled eggs, tomato slices, pimientos, stuffed olives, etc...

POTATO AND CHICKEN SALAD
(Ensalada de Pollo y Papas)

3 lbs. chicken breasts	1 sweet pickle – chopped
1 lb. potatoes	1 can asparagus - drained
2 apples- peeled and diced	½ cup stuffed olives – sliced
1 (8 oz) can small green peas- drained	1 medium onion – finely chopped
1 small can pimiento- chopped	1 cup mayonnaise

Boil chicken with onions and salt. Dice chicken. Peel, dice and boil the potatoes. Mix all ingredients together, adding mayonnaise last. Add pimiento juice as needed. Garnish with boiled eggs, asparagus and pimiento.

GLAZE FOR POTATO SALAD
(Glacé para Ensalada de Papas)

After you have made your potato salad, place in a bowl or in a mold and refrigerate for over two hours. Unmold and spread this glaze over it.

1 envelope unflavored gelatin   1/2 cup cold chicken consommé

Dissolve the gelatin in cold consommé, then heat, stirring until gelatin is dissolved. Let cool, add mayonnaise, beat and let rest for 10 minutes. Spread half of this mixture on unmolded potato salad, place salad again in refrigerate for 10 minutes, then spread more glaze on the salad and leave in refrigerator until ready to serve. Garnish with pimiento slices or green peppers, sliced eggs, sliced olives, etc...

Egg Dishes

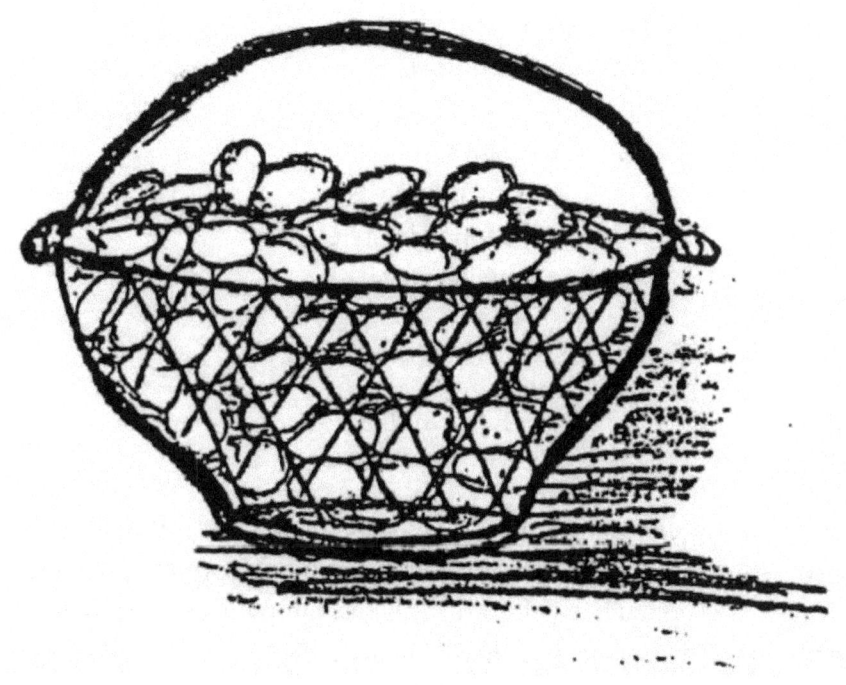

The only thing that endures is
the love of God....

EGG STUFFED POTATOES
(Papas Rellenas con Huevos)

Boil uniform sized, unpeeled potatoes. Let cool down, peel and hollow out, leaving a half inch shell. Drop one raw egg into each potato, sprinkle grated Parmesan, Holland or American cheese on top and bake in a buttered oven tray for 30 minutes at 350' F. Sprinkle with chopped parsley.

EGGS IN A JACKET
(Huevos en Camisa)

4 eggs	capers
2 cups water	stuffed olives
1 tablespoon vinegar	chopped parsley
salt	white sauce

WHITE SAUCE *(for Eggs in Jacket)*

2 tablespoons butter	1 cup milk
1 tablespoon flour	salt and pepper

Melt butter over low heat, add flour and stir until well blended. Slowly add hot milk salt and pepper, stirring until sauce thickens. Poach eggs in boiling water with salt and vinegar until whites are cooked but yolks are still soft. Drop poached eggs into white sauce and top with olives, capers and chopped parsley.

OMELET FOR LENT
(Tortilla de Cuaresma)

8 eggs	2 tablespoons chopped onion
1 (7 1/2 oz) can tuna fish	1 boiled potato, diced

Beat eggs and mix with the other ingredients. Melt butter or oil in omelet pan. Pour omelet into pan, cook on one side and turn to cook the other side.

EGGS MALAGUEÑA
(Huevos a la Malagueña)

6 eggs	1 (6 oz.) can tomato sauce
1 teaspoon salt	1 can asparagus tips – drained
3 slices boiled ham	1 teaspoon chopped onion
1 (6 oz) can small green peas	

Grease small bowls or ramekins with butter or oil. Put 1/2 slice boiled ham on each ramekin. Place 2 eggs over ham, then salt, green peas, chopped onion, 1 tablespoon tomato sauce and asparagus tips over eggs. Bake in 300'F oven until eggs are cooked. (about 30 minutes)

CARIBBEAN OMELET
(Tortilla Caribe)

6 beaten eggs	¼ lb. grated Holland or Edam cheese
1/2 teaspoon salt	1 oz. melted butter
1/2 lb. sandwich bread (remove crusts)	4 tablespoons cooking oil
1 cup milk	Confectioners sugar

Soak bread in hot milk. Beat eggs, add bread, cheese and melted butter. Pour mixture in heated omelet pan with cooking oil, cook one side, turn the omelet and cook the other side. Dust with Confectioners' sugar, invert on a serving plate and dust again with Confectioners' sugar.

SPAGHETTI OMELET
(Tortilla de Espaguetis)

1 cup boiled spaghetti	1 tablespoon sugar
6 eggs	1 tablespoon butter – melted
1 teaspoon salt	Holland or American cheese
1/2 cup milk	

Mix boiled spaghetti, milk, sugar, melted butter and cheese. Beat eggs with salt. Add eggs and mix well. Melt 2 tablespoons butter or vegetable oil in a skillet, add omelet mixture and cook first one side, then turn and cook until done.

ASPARAGUS SOUFFLÉ
(Soufflé de Espárragos)

2 oz. butter (4 tablespoons)
6 tablespoons flour
1 can asparagus tips
6 eggs-separated
1 tablespoon lime juice
1 teaspoon salt
1 1/2 cups warm milk

Make a white sauce with the butter, flour, milk and salt. Add drained asparagus tips. Add beaten egg yolks and lime j u ice. Beat egg whites until foamy and fold into the other mixture. Pour in a greased baking dish placed in a larger pan with about 1 inch deep water. Bake in 350°F oven for 1 hour. Serve immediately.

SWEET OMELET
(Tortilla Dulce)

6 eggs
6 soda crackers- crushed
1/4 teaspoon vanilla
2 tablespoons sugar
1/2 cup Holland or American cheese
salt
1 cup milk

Beat egg whites until foamy, fold in yolks. Add crushed crackers and salt. Mix well and fry in a buttered omelet pan, folding the omelet as it cooks. Drain any butter remaining in the pan and slowly add milk, more butter, vanilla, grated cheese and sugar. Cook on low heat until all the liquid is absorbed.

CHEESE SOUFFLÉ
(Soufflé de Queso)

3 tablespoons butter
1 cup hot milk
1 cup Holland or American cheese

Salt & black pepper
3 eggs - separated

Preheat oven to 475°F. Melt butter. Slowly add hot milk, grated cheese, salt, black pepper and cook over low heat stirring continuously until cheese is melted. Beat egg yolks and add to the milk mixture, stirring continuously and cook until it thickens. Remove from stove and let mixture cool down. Beat egg whites until stiff and fold gently into the cooled mixture. Pour in greased baking dish. Bake for 10 minutes at 475°F, then lower oven temperature to 300'F and bake for 30 minutes. Serve immediately.

GREEN PEA OMELET
(Tortilla de Petit Pois)

6 eggs
1 tablespoon chopped onion
1 (8 oz) can small green peas

2 slices ham – chopped
Butter or oil
Salt

Sauté ham and onion in butter. Turn off heat and add the green peas, well drained. Beat eggs with salt, add ham and pea mixture and mix well. Cook in vegetable oil as you would any other omelet.

HAM OMELET
(Tortilla de Jamón)

Dice several slices boiled ham and 1 small onion and sauté in butter. Prepare mashed potatoes or use left over mashed potatoes. Mix together the ham and the mashed potatoes. Beat eggs, add the filling and chopped parsley. Cook in butter or oil. Sprinkle top with parsley and serve.

Meats

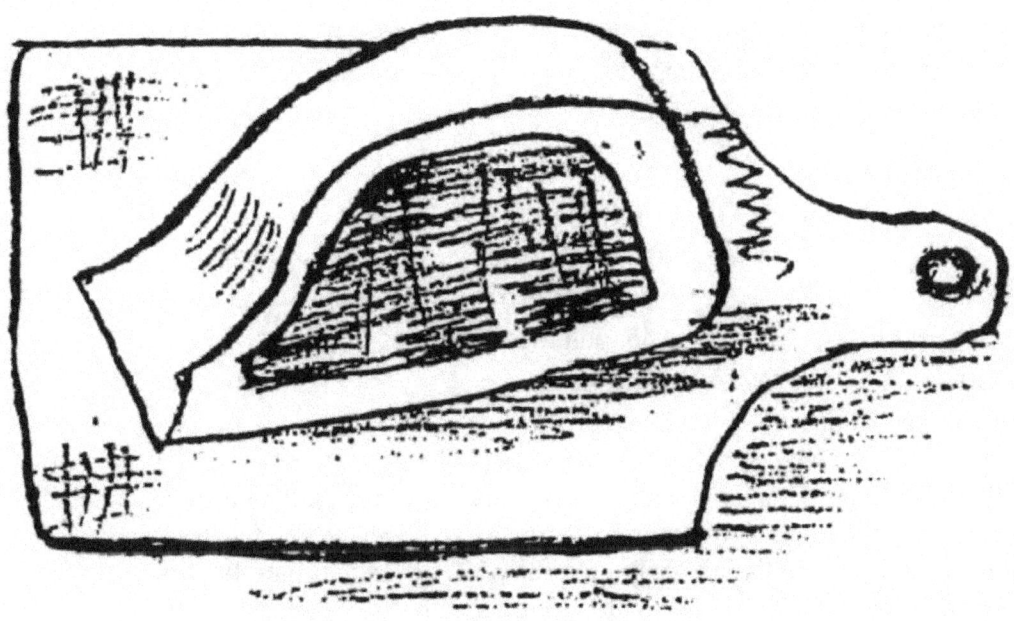

The kitchen is the heart of the home...

BEEF STEAK WITH GREEN PEPPERS
(Biftec con Pimientos Verdes)

3 flank steaks
2 green peppers- chopped
1/4 cup lime juice
3 tablespoons soy sauce
1 tablespoon Worcestershire sauce
1 teaspoon salt
1/3 cup vegetable oil

Marinate meat with all the other ingredients for 6 hours or longer. Remove meat from marinade and drain. Fry peppers in vegetable oil. Remove peppers and in the same frying pan fry the meat. Return peppers to frying pan, heat and serve.

MEAT BALLS "DOÑA VIRGINIA"
(Abondiguitas "doña Virginia)

1 lb. lean ground pork
1 teaspoon salt
1/2 teaspoon nutmeg flour
1 lb. potatoes- diced
1 egg yolk
2 tablespoons olive oil

Mix meat, salt and nutmeg. Shape into small balls, the size of a walnut, and roll in flour. Meanwhile boil the diced potatoes in salted water to cover. When the potatoes start to get tender, drop meatballs in slowly over the potatoes and stir gently with a downward-upward movement so as not to disturb the meatballs or they will break. Let simmer until cooked and the sauce starts to thicken. Beat the egg yolk in a small bowl, add 2 tablespoons olive oil, beat well and add to the meatballs. Stir to mix. Cover and simmer for 30 minutes.

BEEF "MARÍA"
(Biftec de "María")

4 thin tenderloin steaks
2 slices prosciutto ham
2 slices Swiss cheese
1 egg- beaten

Cracker crumbs
3 tablespoons wine
3 tablespoons water

Season meat to taste. Place 1/2 slice ham and 1/2 slice cheese on each steak, roll up and hold with toothpicks. Dip rolls in beaten egg, then in cracker crumbs. Brown rolls in butter or oil. Place in a mold and add water and wine.
Cover and bake in 350°F oven for 20 to 30 minutes. Thicken gravy with cornstarch and add mushrooms or use a gravy mix.

BEEF "INESITA"
(Biftec "Inesita")

6 thin steaks- boneless
1 medium onion-sliced
garlic
orégano
salt

1 egg- beaten
1 tomato- sliced
Vinegar
olive oil

Season meat with garlic, salt and orégano. Mix the egg, vinegar and oil and add to the meat. Add onion and tomato slices and combine with t he meat. Refrigerate, covered, overnight. When ready to use, remove meat from marinade and fry in olive oil or butter. Add the marinade with the onion and the tomato slices. Cook several minutes until onion is transparent.

BEEF STEAK "à la LOLA"
(Filete "a la Lola")

4 thin tenderloin or sirloin boneless steaks	1 bay leaf
3 slices boiled ham	Dash nutmeg
6 stuffed olives	Black pepper
1 teaspoon capers	Salt
1 medium onion- chopped	½ cup dry red wine
1 hard	½ cup water

Grind the boiled ham. Chop the stuffed olives, the hard boiled egg and half the onion. Mix with the ham, capers and seasonings. Place one tablespoon filling on each steak and roll up and hold with toothpicks. Brown in butter. Remove to a platter. Add more butter to the same pan if needed, sauté the other half onion and bay leaf until onion is transparent. Add the meat rolls, meat juices left in the platter, the red dry wine and 1/2 cup water. Simmer, covered for 15 minutes. Add flour or cornstarch to thicken gravy.

HAM LOAF
(Butifarrón de Jamón con Piña)

3 tablespoons butter	1/3 cup green pepper- chopped
1/2 cup brown sugar	2 tablespoons onions- chopped
1 can pineapple slices	1 cup cracker crumbs
maraschino cherries	1/2 teaspoon white pepper
1 1/2 lb. ground boiled ham	2 beaten eggs
1/2 lb. ground pork	2/3 cup milk or half and half

Mix sugar and butter in a loaf pan. Place pan on low heat until the butter and sugar are melted. Turn pan sideways and around to cover sides with syrup. Place pineapple slices and cherries on the bottom and sides of pan. Mix ail the other ingredients and place in the loaf pan without disturbing the pineapple slices. Press down to remove air bubbles. Bake in 375°F oven for 1 hour. Cool and unmold.

STEWED CURED MEAT
(Carne Cecina o Mandurrera)

1 1/2 lbs. cured meat	1 teaspoon chopped garlic
3 tablespoons oil	2 green peppers- chopped
1 lb. tomatoes- chopped	1 tablespoon tomato sauce
2 onions- sliced	1 bay leaf

Soak meat for several hours or overnight. Cut meat in pieces and boil until tender. Drain and flake meat. Sauté onion, garlic, tomatoes, peppers, tomato sauce and bay leaf in olive oil. Add flaked meat and mix, adding water if necessary. Cook for 20 or 30 minutes. Garnish with pimiento slices, green peas and sliced hard boiled eggs. Or you can add 6 beaten eggs and cook as you would cook scrambled eggs.

KID OR GOAT "PACA"
(Cabrito a la Cazadora "Paca")

Cut meat in serving pieces. Place in a large pot. Add salt to taste. Add to the pot:

1 tablespoon black peppercorns	1 lb. small onions
2 whole garlic heads-unpeeled	stuffed olives
3 tablespoons shortening or oil	3 bay leaves

Cook, covered, over low heat. When meat is almost tender, add:

2 cans anchovies	vinegar to taste

Simmer for 20 to 30 minutes. Turn heat off and let rest to blend flavors.

SWEET AND SOUR PORK "DOÑA JUANA"
(Cerdo Agridulce "doña Juana")

1 pork shoulder (about 8 lbs.)	½ teaspoon ground cloves
1 cup sugar	Juice of 2 limes

Season meat and refrigerate overnight. Set meat in oven pan, sprinkle with sugar, ground cloves and lime juice. Bake in 350°F oven (25 minutes per pound). You can also use any other cut of pork without bone, or a pork loin.

BEEF CUTLETS
(Coteletes)

4 sirloin steaks- boneless	2 beaten eggs
1 tomato- sliced	2 tablespoons Parmesan cheese
1 onion- sliced	1/2 teaspoon salt
parsley- chopped	cracker meal
4 tablespoons olive oil	margarine or butter

Cut diagonal gashes on both sides of the steaks, as you would for a baked ham. Place meat in a platter with tomato, onion, parsley, olive oil, Parmesan cheese, salt and beaten eggs. Turn to coat all sides. Refrigerate, covered, over-night. Drain meat and roll in cracker meal. Fry in margarine or butter.

CAROL'S PORK CHOPS
(Chuletas "Carol")

3 (16 oz) cans Pork and Beans	3 lbs. pork chops
3/4 cup catsup	1 lb. sliced bacon
1/2 cup brown sugar	¾ cup sliced onions

Season pork chops. Empty beans into a large oven proof mold. Add catsup, sugar and onions. Place pork chops over beans, then cover with bacon slices. Bake in a 350' oven for 1 to 1 1/2 hours.

***About Pork Offal.** The next recipe is considered a savory delicacy in Puerto Rico and many Caribbean countries. It's nutritious & economical. Please read before moving on.*

There are many definitions for the word OFFAL. In this context the Cambridge English Dictionary definition is used, meaning the organs inside an animal, such as the brain, the heart, and the liver, eaten as food. Gandinga is a word of African roots used in Puerto Rico to describe a stew made with organ beef or pork meats

PORK OFFAL
(Gandinga de Cerdo)

3 lbs. pork offal (liver, heart, kidneys)	stuffed olives
2 tablespoons vinegar	1 lb. potatoes
sofrito- (see index)	1 can pimiento
1/2 cup red dry wine	bay leaves
1/2 cup beer	3 tablespoons tomato sauce

Wash pork offal in water, add 2 tablespoons vinegar, or you can use lemon or lime juice. Cut meats in pieces. Place all the ingredients in a pot over high heat, stirring until it boils. Turn to medium heat, cover pot and cook for about 1 hour. Add cubed potatoes and cook until potatoes are tender. Do not let the juices dry out. If necessary, add more beer or water.

YUCCA TURNOVERS
(Empanadas de Yuca)

DOUGH
10 lbs. yucca
annato oil
Garlic salt

Grate yucca. Add annato oil and garlic salt. You will add juices from the meat filling as to form a smooth paste.

FILLING
5 lbs. ground pork, beef or ½ & ½
Sofrito (see index for recipe)
1 can tomato sauce
1 can pimentos - sliced
raisins
Stuffed olives
4 hard boiled eggs - sliced
Wilted banana leaves

Cook meat with sofrito, tomato sauce, olives and raisins. Add salt, pepper and orégano. Add broth or water to make a juicy stew, as you will add some of the meat juices to the grated yucca to make a smooth paste. You can also add milk. On a wilted banana leaf, about 12" × 12", spoon annato oil and meat juices from the meat filling. Spoon yucca on leaf, spread into a rectangle, top with 1 or 2 tablespoons filling, a slice of boiled egg, and strips of pimiento. Fold leaf to wrap the yucca over the filling, leaving ends of leaf open. Place turnovers in one layer on a shallow oven pan. Bake in 375' F oven for 45 minutes, turning once. These turnovers freeze well. If baked while still frozen, bake for 75 minutes. (Makes 24 turnovers)

BREADED PIG'S FEET
(Patas de Cerdo Empanizadas)

2 lbs. fresh pig's feet	2 – 3 garlic cloves
2 tablespoons salt	1 bay leaf
3 quarts water or more, to cover meat	3 whole cloves
2 or 3 large onions	1 cup white dry wine

BREADING INGREDIENTS

flour	chopped parsley
eggs	salt

Boil pig's feet until tender with all the other ingredients, except breading ingredients. Drain and cool. Remove the bones and cut the pig's feet in large pieces. Roll in flour, then dip in beaten eggs seasoned with salt and chopped parsley. Fry in deep oil. The front feet are considered a better choice.

BAKED HAM
(Jamón al Horno)

1 (12 lbs.) ham	2 tablespoons whole cloves
1 lb. brown sugar	2 cups cooking wine
2 tablespoons mustard	1 teaspoon ground cloves

Mix brown sugar, ground cloves and mustard. Score the ham, make shallow, diagonal cuts on top of the ham and push whole cloves at each Intersection. Bake in hot 425°F oven for 10 minutes, or until the diagonal cuts open. Remove from the oven and glaze with the sugar mixture. Pour wine over ham. Return to oven for 1 1/2 hours, basting often. Decorate with pineapple slices and maraschino cherries.

COLD EYE of ROUND ROAST
(Lechón de Res en Fiambre)

1 (3 to 4 lbs.) eye of the round	1 large onion – sliced
3 teaspoons salt	1 whole garlic head
1 teaspoon black pepper	1 – 2 bay leaves
4 carrots	8 whole cloves

Season meat with salt and pepper. Refrigerate, covered, overnight. Boil the meat in water to cover, with all the other ingredients, correct salt and boil until the meat is tender. Remove meat from liquid, drain and cool. Wrap meat in aluminum foil and refrigerate until ready to use.

SAUCE for the Meat

1 cup white vinegar	1 tablespoon capers
1 tablespoon peppercorns	2 tablespoons caper liquid
2 sour pickles- sliced	1 cup olive oil
2 sweet pickles- sliced	

Mix all ingredients together and refrigerate. When ready to serve, slice meat very thin and pour the sauce over meat. Lest rest to blend flavors.

SAVORY MEAT LOAF
(Meat Loaf Sabroso)

1 1/2 lbs. ground beef	1 teaspoon salt
3/4 lb. bulk sausage	1/2 teaspoon orégano
1 cup oatmeal- uncooked	1 teaspoon basil- chopped
1 medium onion- chopped	1/4 teaspoon black pepper
1/2 cup parsley- chopped	1 cup V8 or tomato juice
2 beaten eggs	4 slices bacon

Mix well but handle lightly all ingredients. Place in a greased loaf pan or shape into a roll and cover with the bacon slices. Pour V8 or tomato juice over the loaf. Bake in 400' F oven for 15 minutes, then at 350° F for 45 minutes. Baste occasionally adding more liquid if necessary.

RAGGED MEAT STEW
(Ropa Vieja)

2 lbs. beef	2 tablespoons olive oil
2 tomatoes- chopped	2 tablespoons capers
2 green peppers- chopped	Chopped garlic
2 onions- thinly sliced	salt

Boil meat as to make a soup stock. Remove meat from broth and pull apart in shreds, with fingers. Season with salt and chopped garlic. Sauté tomatoes, onions, and green peppers in olive oil. Add shredded meat and capers. Simmer stirring often. Serve on a platter with boiled potatoes and garbanzos. You may add cabbage, carrots and other- vegetables of your choice.

*The word **Ragged** is used to describe the appearance of the meat, old and tattered, as it's pulled into strips. The literal translation of this dish is "Old Clothes".*

PORK MEAT ROLL
(Rollo de Carne de Cerdo)

1 lb. ground pork	1 1/2 teaspoon black pepper
1/2 lb. ground ham	24 soda crackers- ground
1 1/2 teaspoons nutmeg	3 eggs
1 1/2 teaspoons salt	1 can foie gras (goose liver)
2 tablespoons Worcestershire sauce	

Mix all ingredients together, form into a roll and place in greased oven proof pan. Bake in 350' F oven for 45 minutes. You can add 2 or 3 tablespoons wine.

OUR VERY OWN STUFFED CHEESE
(Nuestro Queso Relleno)

1 ball Holland or Edam cheese (3-3 ½ lbs.)	Culantro, chopped
3 ½ lbs. chicken pieces	¼ teaspoon oregano
2 tablespoons sofrito	¼ cup cooking wine
2 tablespoons olive oil	12 stuffed olives, sliced
2 tablespoons tomato sauce	2 tablespoons raisins
2 bay leaves	1 large potato, diced, parboiled
cilantro- chopped	2 hard boiled eggs, cubed or diced
long leaf	1 tsp salt
	1 can pimentos

Scrape the paraffin covering the cheese. After you scrape, to remove all the paraffin, dip the ball of cheese in hot water, remove immediately and wipe with a paper towel. Cut a slice off the top of the ball, a 3 to 4 inches circle, large enough to allow to scoop out the cheese, using a teaspoon, and leaving a shell about 1/4 inch thick. Save the piece you cut off to be used later as a lid. Cut the uncooked chicken meat in one inch cubes, discarding bones and skin. Sauté chicken meat in olive oil adding all the other ingredients, except the boiled eggs, and cook until meat is tender. If not juicy, add chicken broth or water. Correct salt, on the low side, because the cheese is salty. Soak the cheese in a bowl with cold tap water to cover and inside the cheese, about 1 or 2 hours. Discard the water, place the cheese in a mold lined with a banana leaf, if available. If a banana leaf is not available, line the mold with lightly greased aluminum foil. Spoon the filling into the cheese ball, alternating with pieces of chopped eggs. On top, place the reserved piece of cheese you cut off the top. Cover with another piece of banana leaf or with a piece of greased aluminum foil. It is traditional to use a banana leaf as it enhances the flavor of this dish and keeps the cheese from sticking to the mold. Bake in hot 350' F oven for 1 hour. Remove from oven, remove the banana leaf, place a large plate, inverted over the mold, and carefully flip both around. Remove the mold and the banana leaf or aluminum foil. Cut in pie shaped wedges and serve immediately as cheese gets hard when cold.

To make a SIMPLE SOFRITO:
Sauté 1 finely chopped onion, ½ cup culantro, cilantro or parsley, 1 green pepper & 5 – 6 cloves of crushed garlic in 2 tablespoons olive oil. When tender add 1 tablespoon (about ½ can) tomato paste and stir to mix. This mixture holds refrigerated for 3 days & frozen for 1 month.

STUFFED LEG OF PORK "TÍA BEBÉ"
(Pierna de Cerdo Tía Bebé)

1 (6 to 8 lbs.) leg of pork

Remove the bone, cutting around the bone with a paring knife, starting at the widest part, cutting around and separating meat away from the bone. Or make a long cut on the thinner side of the leg until you reach the bone, then cut around the bone, and you will get an almost flat piece of meat. Season with 1 teaspoon salt for each pound of meat, 2 teaspoons minced garlic, black pepper and 2 tablespoons vinegar.

FILLING

1/2 lb. ground boiled ham
1 cup French bread- soaked in milk
1 medium onion- chopped
1 tablespoon butter
1 can foie gras (canned duck or chicken)

Sauté onion in butter until transparent. Mix all the other ingredients together and place in the hollowed out leg of pork. Sew all openings with a long needle and strong thread. Rub the meat with annato oil or with cooking oil. Bake in 350' F oven (25 minutes per pound). Serve cold, thinly sliced. Serve side dishes of apple sauce.

CABBAGE PIE "MARINA"
(Pastelón de Repollo "Marina")

1 cabbage head
1 lb. ground beef
1 can tomato sauce
1 teaspoon orégano
1 green pepper- chopped
1 medium onion- chopped
1 envelope Sazón
stuffed olives
1 can pimiento - sliced
2 hard boiled eggs- sliced
1 teaspoon salt
chicken or beef consommé

Core the cabbage and boil, separating the leaves, until wilted but not too soft. Cook meat with the other ingredients and about ½ can tomato sauce. Remove the thick vein in the cabbage leaves. Line the bottom and sides of a greased oven proof mold with half the cabbage leaves. Spoon filling over the cabbage leaves, cover with the reserved cabbage leaves, pressing gently to compact. Dilute the reserved tomato sauce with broth and pour over the first layer of leaves, then the filling, cabbage leaves again, etc... To serve, cut in wedges.

STUFFED PIMENTOS "SALAZAR"
(Pimientos Morrones Rellenos "Salazar")

1 lb. ground pork	1 teaspoon parsley- chopped
1 teaspoon nutmeg	1 can tomato sauce
1 teaspoon salt	1 tablespoon olive oil
1 beaten egg	canned pimientos (reserve liquid)
1/4 cup ground almonds	

Mix meat, salt, nutmeg, egg, half the almonds and chopped parsley. Stuff pimientos with the filling, pressing to compact meat.

BATTER

Mix 1/2 cup flour   ½ cup water seasoned with salt

Dip each pimiento in batter and fry in oil, one at a time, turning until the coating is cooked. Place close together in a glass mold. Mix pimiento juice, 1 tablespoon olive oil, reserved almonds and I can tomato sauce and pour over pimientos. Bake in 375' oven for 40 minutes.

ROAST BEEF "OLGA AND CELIA"
(Rosbif Asado estilo "Olga y Celia")

1 beef fillet	2 tablespoons butter
salt	1 cup red dry wine
chopped garlic	1 can mushrooms
cooking oil or butter	1 bay leaf
	1 teaspoon flour

Season meat with salt and garlic. Rub well with oil or butter. Cover and refrigerate overnight. When ready to use drain marinade and broil meat, turning as necessary, until it browns and is cooked to your taste. In a frying pan make a gravy with the butter, wine, seasonings to your- taste, bay leaf, mushrooms and flour. Do not overcook. Add the meat marinade and meat drippings. Cut the meat in thin slices and serve with the gravy. BON APETIT! ! !

COLD ROAST BEEF IN "DEER" MARINADE
(Roast Beef Fiambre en Adobe de Ciervo)

3 lbs. eye of the round roast

"DEER" MARINADE

2 onions- sliced	1 bay leaf
1 cup white wine	14 oz. cooking ham (tocino) – diced
1/4 cup white vinegar	2 teaspoons salt
2 garlic cloves	

In a glass or enameled pan, place meat and marinade. Refrigerate, covered, for 3 days, turning often. Sauté diced ham in butter. Add drained meat and brown, turning often. Add wine and enough water or consommé to cover meat. Boil briskly for 30 minutes, turning meat often. Remove meat and refrigerate, covered, for at least 6 hours. To serve, slice thinly.

LYONNAISE SAUSAGE "MAMI"
(Salchichón Lionés "Mami")

¾ lb. ground pork	**BREADING**
1/2 lb. ground lean ham	cracker meal
3 beaten eggs	eggs
2 cups cracker meal	
1/4 teaspoon nutmeg	
salt	

Mix all ingredients together and shape into two rolls. Roll in beaten eggs, then in cracker meal. Have ready a deep pot with boiling salted water. Brown the rolls in hot cooking oil. Remove rolls and drop, gently, into the boiling water and boil for 1 1/2 hours, turning occasionally. Remove rolls from water and drain well. When the rolls have cooled, wrap in aluminum foil and refrigerate. Serve cold, sliced thin.

STEAK AND BEER
(Steak con Cerveza)

1 1/2 lbs. steak of your choice
1 1/2 cups beer- at room temperature
1/2 cup onions- sliced
3 tablespoons soy sauce

1 tablespoon sugar
1 tablespoon garlic – chopped
1/3 cup vegetable oil

Marinate meat in all the other ingredients. Refrigerate covered, for 6 hours or overnight. Drain well, reserving marinade. Brown meat in hot oil, turning once. Remove meat to a warm platter. Add all the marinade liquid to the same pan and cook stirring often. You may thicken the gravy with one tablespoon cornstarch.. Pour gravy over meat.

Poultry

Our memories bring roses in
December and stars in our darkest nights...

GUINEA HEN IN CHOCOLATE GRAVY "MAMA CHITA"
(Guinea en Salsa de Chocolate "Mamá Chita")

Make a good stew with a guinea hen, salt, black pepper, garlic, onions, bay leaves, green peppers, cilantro leaves and olive oil. You can use your own recipe, adding ingredients to your taste; everything except tomato sauce. When chicken is tender add 1 or 2 bars chocolate (1 or 2 ounces)- Menier, Cortes, or a similar one. Simmer a little while longer. Chocolate scorches very easily, so watch your pot and make sure you have it on the lowest heat. If the gravy dries out, add water or chicken consommé.

STUFFED CHICKEN LEGS
(Musios de Pollo Rellenos con Jamón)

6 chicken legs

STUFFING

1 cup chopped onions	1/3 cup chopped parsley
1/2 cup mushroom pieces	¼ cup dry Vermouth
1 teaspoon chopped garlic	1 teaspoon thyme
3 tablespoons butter	Salt
3/4 lb. ground ham	Black pepper

Bone chicken legs but do not remove skin. Season to taste. Simmer onion in butter for 8 to 10 minutes. Add ground ham, stir, add all the other ingredients, stirring often. Remove from stove. When stuffing is cool, stuff the chicken legs.. Sew or tie the ends. Fry in butter or cooking oil.

CHICKEN PORTA COELI
(Pollo "Porta Coeli")

4 chicken pieces- seasoned	1 cup cooking wine
olive oil for frying	2 bay leaves

Fry seasoned chicken in the olive oil until browned. Add bay leaves and wine. Cover and simmer, turning often, until the chicken is cooked and golden.

CHICKEN STUFFED WITH "MOFONGO"
(Pollo Relleno con Mofongo)

1 (3 1/2 to 4 lbs.) whole chicken	½ teaspoon oregano
4 teaspoons salt	Black pepper
1 teaspoon ground garlic	

"MOFONGO"

2 or 3 green plantains	Salt
6 slices bacon	Olive oil
chopped garlic	

Peel the plantains, cut in one inch diagonal slices and fry in deep oil or fat. Mash in a mortar or grind in a meat grinder. Season with salt. Add the chopped garlic and chopped bacon. Season the chicken with salt, garlic, orégano and black pepper. Stuff the chicken through the tail opening. Close opening with poultry pins. Bake in hot oven, 350' F for 1 to 1 1/2 hours or until done. You may cover chicken with aluminum foil for about half of the cooking time, then uncover to brown.

You may use rice and pigeon peas (garbanzos) instead of "Mofongo" in which case you will cook the rice and pigeon peas only until partially cooked, and using only 2 slices chopped bacon in the stuffing. Place 2 whole bacon slices over the chicken and bake until done.

STUFFED TURKEY
(Pavo Trufado)

1 (12 lb) turkey
salt - 1 teaspoon per pound

STUFFING

6 lbs. ground pork
6 lbs. ground ham
2 cans foie grás (goose or chicken liver paté)
ground black pepper

ground nutmeg
12 beaten eggs
salt

BASTING INGREDIENTS

½ cup vegetable oil
2 – 3 cups wine

Wash the turkey. With a sharp paring knife cut along the back of the fowl, from the neck to the tail, cutting only skin and meat. Do not cut into bone. Separate skin and meat from bones, working around until all the meat is separated from the carcass. When you reach the wings and the thighs, cut through the joints, leaving the bones attached to the meat. That is, do not remove bones from wings and thighs. Sew up gashes on the body, using needle and strong thread, leaving an opening along the back, about 4 to 5 inches long. Season the bird with salt, pepper and nutmeg. Refrigerate while preparing stuffing. Mix together all stuffing ingredients. Fill turkey with the stuffing, pushing the mixture into the crop and into the cavity. Do not pack too firmly since stuffing expands while cooking. Sew opening. Roll and knead the bird to get rid of air bubbles and make the stuffing more compact. Place the bird in a greased deep roasting pan. Pour cooking oil and the wine over the turkey. Cover pan and bake in a 325' F oven for 3 to 3 1/2 hours, basting often. Uncover for the last hour to brown meat. Remove from the oven and when cool enough to handle, remove turkey to a platter. Wrap in plastic wrap or aluminum foil and refrigerate. Strain the juices. The curdles make a very flavorful spread to eat with crackers. The stuffed turkey is eaten cold. Remove the thread used to sew the fowl by pulling gently. With a large carving knife cut the turkey from the neck all the way through the breast and down to the tail. You will have two halves. Slice each half across in 1/4 inch slices. Arrange slices overlapping on a platter. Decorate with parsley or fruits of your choice. Serve with cranberry sauce, whole cranberries, mint jelly, and apple sauce.

CHICKEN BREAST "REBECCA"
(Pechugas de Pollo "Rebeca")

4 chicken breasts or other pieces	1 can Cream of Chicken Soup
Pancake Mix or Presto flour	1 can evaporated milk
1 envelope Onion soup mix	2 tablespoons Parmesan cheese

Coat the chicken pieces with the flour. Place in oven proof dish. In a separate bowl mix onion soup, mushroom soup and evaporated milk. Pour over chicken. Bake, covered for 1 hour in 350' F oven. Add Parmesan cheese and bake for 15 minutes longer.

CHICKEN STUFFED WITH VEGETABLES
(Pollo Relleno con Vegetales)

1 (4 lbs.) whole chicken	1 onion – chopped
2 tablespoons salt	1 medium potato – diced
1/2 teaspoon orégano	1 carrot – sliced
1 teaspoon chopped garlic	1 green pepper – cut up
1 tablespoon olive oil	Other vegetables of your choice

Season chicken with salt, orégano and garlic. Mix all the other ingredients together and spoon into the chicken. Bake, covered in 350' F oven for 1 1/2 hours. Uncover for the last 1/2 hour to brown the meat.

CHICKEN A LA "JULIE"
(Pollo a la "Julie")

5 lbs. seasoned chicken pieces

SAUCE

1 onion- chopped	1 1/2 teaspoons nutmeg
3/4 cup water	3/4 teaspoon mustard
3 tablespoons butter	1 can tomato sauce
1 1/2 tablespoons Worcestershire sauce	

Cook onion in butter. Add all the other ingredients and simmer for 10 minutes. Place the chicken in oven dish and pour sauce over the chicken. Bake, covered, in 350' F oven for 1 hour.

CHICKEN IN ONION AND EGG SAUCE "Tía Rita"
(Pollo en Pepitoria "Tía Rita")

4 chicken breasts	¼ lb. butter
1 lb. onions- sliced	2 egg yolks
3 tablespoons chopped parsley	

Boil chicken breasts until tender in water to cover, with salt, 1 onion and 1 large sprig parsley. Remove chicken, reserve broth. Flake chicken meat with fingers, discarding bones and skin. In a large skillet cook sliced onions in butter, over very low heat, until onion is transparent. Do not brown onion. Add the flaked chicken meat and stir well.

In a small bowl or cup, beat the egg yolks, add some hot chicken broth, and add to the chicken, cooking over low heat for several minutes, stirring continuously. Add more broth if necessary. Serve as entree or as "hor d'oeuvres".

CHICKEN SURPRISES
(Sorpresas de Pollo)

6 boned chicken breasts	**STUFFING**
Seasonings (salt, orégano, garlic, cumin)	6 slices boiled ham
2 lbs. sliced bacon	6 slices Swiss cheese
	1 small can pimentos - sliced
	4 hard boiled eggs - chopped

BREADING

4 beaten eggs	**1 cup cracker meal**

Pound chicken breasts until thin. Season. On each chicken breast place 1 slice ham, 1 slice cheese, 1 tablespoon chopped egg and pimiento strips. Roll tightly, then wrap in bacon slices and secure with toothpicks. Dip in beaten eggs and roll in cracker meal. Brown rolls in hot oil. Place rolls in oven dish and bake, covered, in 350' F oven for 45 minutes. You may add white wine. Can also be cooked in a covered skillet, adding white wine and cornstarch to make gravy. Canned Cream of Chicken soup or Cream of Celery soup make a nice gravy also.

Fish and Sea Food

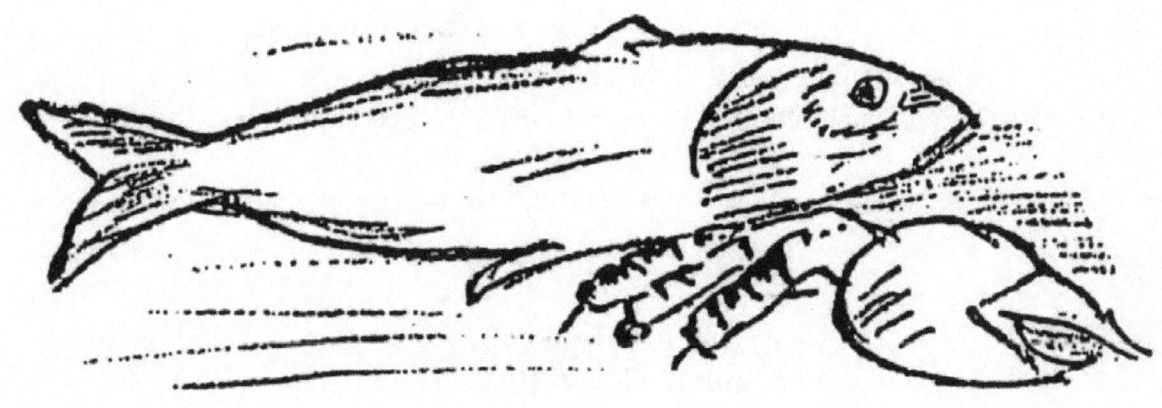

Motherhood is
an agreement with God...

BONITO ROLL
(Brazo de Gitana de Bonito)

2 lbs. potatoes- boiled, skin on
1/2 lb. cream cheese

FILLING
2 cans bonito in olive oil
2 tablespoons sweet chiles or green peppers
Tabasco
2 tablespoons small green peas
3 tablespoons Parmesan cheese

Peel the potatoes while still hot and mash with the cream cheese. In a separate bowl, mix filling ingredients. Spread the mashed potatoes on a piece of wax paper forming a rectangle. Spoon the filling over the potatoes and sprinkle Parmesan cheese on top. Roll as for jelly roll. Pinch ends of wax paper. Refrigerate. Serve cold, over lettuce leaves.
Note: Bonito is like tuna fish. If canned bonito is not available, use canned tuna fish.

SHRIMP IN GARLIC SAUCE
(Camarones al Ajillo)

1 lb. boiled shrimps
3 teaspoons chopped garlic
12 tablespoons butter

Cook garlic in butter over low heat, add shrimps and simmer for 12 to 15 minutes.

SHRIMP SCAMPI
(Camarones Scampi)

Just add dry white wine to the "Shrimp in Garlic Sauce" and simmer.

CODFISH STOMACH "MINA"
(Buches de Bacalao "Mina")

1 lb. dry codfish stomach	2 tablespoons capers
1/2 cup olive oil	½ cup olives
3 onions- chopped	1 can whole tomatoes
2 green peppers - chopped	3 tablespoons almonds
1 small can tomato sauce	3 tablespoons raisins
1 small can pimientos	Dry white wine
	Garbanzo beans - optional

Soak codfish stomach overnight, changing the water several times. Cut codfish stomach in pieces. In a large pot, with olive oil, cook all the other ingredients, over low heat. Add the codfish stomach and simmer for 1 hour. Let rest before serving. Note: Codfish stomach comes dry and salted and is available in Spanish markets. It is very expensive today.

PETIT AIOLI WITH CODFISH AND VEGETABLES
(Petit Aioli con Bacalao y Vegetales)

1 lb. salt codfish	1 bay leaf
parsley	1 green pepper
thyme	

Soak the salt codfish in water to cover, for several hours or overnight, changing the water several times. Simmer for 12 minutes with the seasonings. Remove codfish and flake. Have ready the following ingredients:

boiled potatoes	boiled string beans
boiled garbanzos	asparagus tips
boiled carrots	hard boiled eggs- sliced
boiled cauliflower	lemon slices

On a large serving platter, arrange the flaked codfish, the vegetables and the sliced eggs. Decorate with lemon slices and serve with the Petit Aioli.

PETIT AIOLI *(for Codfish and Vegetables)*

2 teaspoons chopped garlic	Salt
2 egg yolks	Black pepper
1/2 teaspoon lime or lemon juice	1 cup olive oil

Beat yolks until creamy. Add garlic, salt, black pepper and lemon juice. Beat until lemon colored. In a thin stream, add olive oil, beating constantly until thickened like mayonnaise.

SHRIMP CREOLE
(Camarones a la Criolla)

1/2 lb. boiled shrimps	1/2 cup water
1 medium onion- chopped	1 bay leaf
1 garlic clove- chopped	1 teaspoon cilantro – chopped
1 green pepper- chopped	¼ teaspoon oregano
4 tablespoons butter or olive oil	¼ teaspoon black pepper
4 oz. tomato sauce	1 can pimentos

Over low heat, cook seasonings in olive oil or butter, add tomato sauce, peeled boiled shrimps and water. Simmer for to 15 minutes. Serve with boiled white rice.

COLD SALMON
(Fiambre de Salmón)

2 cans salmon- drained	1 teaspoon salt
2 cups cracker meal	1 teaspoon white pepper
1 onion- chopped	2 eggs- beaten
2 tablespoons lime juice	1 1/3 cups milk
4 tablespoons butter- melted	

Mash salmon, add cracker meal, onion, lime juice, butter, salt and white pepper. Beat eggs, add milk and mix with the other ingredients. Pour in well buttered oven mold. Bake in 375' F oven for 45 minutes. Let stand until cool. Refrigerate and serve with Tartar Sauce. (Recipe on next page)

SALMON SOUFFLÉ
(Flan de Salmón)

1 can Pink salmon	2 garlic cloves
1 can small green peas	1 tablespoon parsley – chopped
1/2 can pimientos	4 eggs – separated
1/4 cup milk	2 teaspoons salt
3 tablespoons cracker meal	¼ teaspoon white pepper
1 onion- chopped	

Drain salmon, remove skin and bones. Grind salmon, green peas, pimientos, onion and garlic. Mix well. Add milk, cracker meal, parsley and egg yolks, one at a time, mixing well after each addition. Beat egg whites until stiff and fold into the salmon mixture. Pour into buttered soufflé pan. Place the soufflé pan into a larger pan with water about 1 inch deep. Bake for 1 hour in 300" F oven.
Serve with home made mayonnaise.

TARTAR SAUCE
(Salsa de Tártar)

1 cup mayonnaise	3 tablespoons chopped pickles
2 tablespoons chopped onion	1 teaspoon chopped parsley

Mix all ingredients together. Serve cold

FISH PUDDING "TÍO PEPE"
(Pudín de Pescado "Tío Pepe")

1 lb. fish	1 tablespoon vegetable oil
5 or 6 eggs- beaten	1 (6 oz.) can tomato paste
3 tablespoons butter- melted	

Boil fish in salted water to cover. Grind fish, add beaten eggs, tomato paste, butter and vegetable oil. Mix well and correct salt. You may also add ground black pepper. Pour in greased baking dish, set in a larger pan with 1 inch of water. Bake in 350' F oven for 1 hour. Let stand to cool and unmold. Refrigerate. Serve with home made mayonnaise.

TUNA PIE "GUARO"
(Pastelón de Atún "Guaro")

2 1/2 lbs. yautía (tanier)
3 tablespoons butter
1 cup hot milk

FILLING

2 cans tuna fish or 1 can salmon	½ small can tomato sauce
1 green pepper- chopped	Salt – pepper – oregano
1 onion- chopped	8 stuffed olives –sliced
long leaf culantro or chopped cilantro	1 small can pimentos – sliced
2 tablespoons olive oil	2 hard boiled eggs - sliced
	2 tablespoons Parmesan cheese

Boil peeled yautía in salted water. While yautía cooks, over low heat cook filling ingredients, except tuna fish and hard boiled eggs. Turn heat off, add tuna fish and stir to mix. Mash yautía with hot milk and butter. Spread half of the yautía on a buttered oven pan and up the sides of the mold about 1 inch. Spoon tuna filling over yautía. Place sliced eggs over filling and cover with a layer of yautía. Smooth the top with a spoon dipped in butter or milk. Sprinkle Parmesan cheese on top. Bake in 350' F oven for 20 to 30 minutes and golden on top.

FISH PUDDING "IRMA"
(Pudín de Pescado "Irma")

1 lb. fish	4 slices white bread
4 oz. butter- melted	1/2 cup milk
6 egg yolks	1/2 teaspoon black pepper
1 egg white	

Boil fish in water to cover with salt. Remove skin and bones. Soak bread in milk and grind together with boiled fish. Add t he egg yolks, egg white, me l ted butter, and pepper. Correct salt and mix well Pour in well buttered baking dish. Top with bread crumbs or Corn Flakes crumbs. Set the baking dish in a larger pan with about l inch of water. Bake in 350' F oven for 1 1/2 hours.

BAKED FISH JARDINIÈRE "ARACELI"
(Pescado a la Jardinera "Araceli")

1 (8 to 10 lb) whole fish	1/2 cup olive oil
1 lb. potatoes- sliced and parboiled	1/4 cup vinegar
1 small can sliced carrots	1/4 cup white wine
4 sweet pickles- sliced	orégano - parsley
1 (8 oz) can tomato sauce	salt- black pepper
stuffed olives	1 onion- chopped
green peppers- sliced	other vegetables of your choice
1 can pimientos- sliced	3 hard boiled eggs sliced

Clean and season the fish. Place fish in a large greased oven pan. Mix all the filling ingredients together except the hard boiled eggs. Spoon into the fish cavity and around fish. Pour tomato sauce, olive oil and wine over the fish. Bake, covered for 1 hour in 350°F oven, basting often. Garnish with egg slices before serving

CODFISH PUDDING
(Pudín de Bacalao)

2 lbs. salt codfish	1 tablespoon cooking oil
1 (6 oz) can tomato paste	or melted butter
10 eggs- beaten	black pepper

Boil salt codfish changing the water several times, or soak overnight and boil for 12 minutes. Grind codfish and mix well with the other ingredients. Pour in greased oven dish, set in a larger pan with about 1 inch water, and bake in 350' F oven for 1 hour. Remove from oven, let stand to cool and unmold. Garnish with pimientos, green peppers, parsley, stuffed olives. Serve with home made mayonnaise.

TUNA FISH OR SALMON PUDDING WITH CORN FLAKES
(Pudín de Atún o Salmón y Corn Flakes)

3 cups Corn Flakes	1 tablespoons chopped parsley
1 1/2 cups hot milk	1 chopped onion
1 tablespoon lime juice	4 eggs
2/3 cup milk cream or half and half	Salt
2 cups boiled tuna or salmon	Black pepper

Soak Corn Flakes in hot milk for 10 minutes. Mix lime juice with half and half or milk cream. Let stand for 10 minutes. Stir both mixtures together. Grind boiled fish and add to the Corn Flakes mixture. Add parsley, onion, salt and pepper to taste. Add eggs, one at a time, beating well after each addition. Pour in greased oven pan. Bake in 375' F oven for 40 minutes. Let stand and when cool, unmold and refrigerate. Serve with home made mayonnaise.

Vegetables

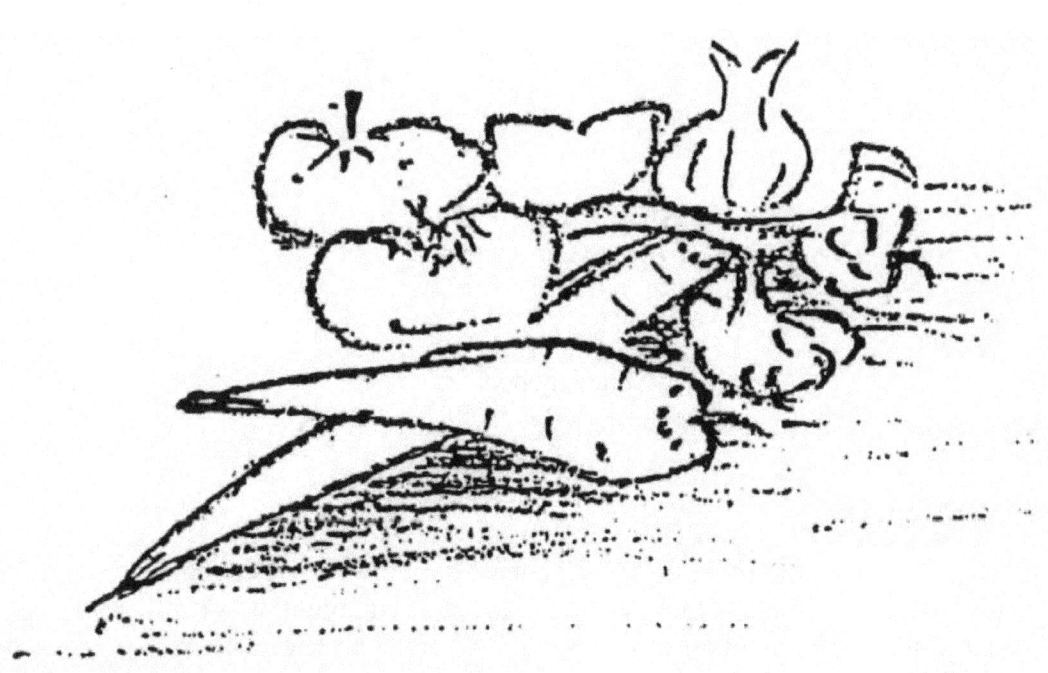

Put your soul in your chores...

SCRAMBLED MERLITONES
(Alboronía de Chayotes)

3 merlitones (chayotes)	salt
1/2 cup sofrito	olive oil
6 beaten eggs	

Cut merlitones lengthwise in 4 pieces and boil in salted water until tender. Peel and dice, discarding fibrous core. Cook sofrito in olive oil, add diced merlitones, stirring well. Beat eggs, season with salt and pour over merlitones, stirring mixture until eggs are cooked but not dry.

BAKED EGGPLANT WITH CHEESE
(Berenjenas al Horno con Queso)

2 medium eggplants	salt
2 tomatoes	black pepper
1 cup Cottage cheese	orégano
2 eggs	Paprika
1/2 cup Mozzarella cheese	

Peel and slice eggplants. Boil in very little salted water. Chop tomatoes. Beat eggs and Cottage cheese together. In a buttered oven dish spread alternating layers of eggplant, egg and Cottage cheese mixture and grated Mozzarella cheese. Bake in 350° F oven for 45 minutes.

GLAZED CARROTS
(Zanahorias Glacé)

2 lbs. small carrots	2 tablespoons butter
3 tablespoons orange juice	½ teaspoon ground ginger
grated lemon peel	¼ cup sugar

Boil carrots in lightly salted water. Melt butter, add sugar, orange juice, lemon peel and ginger to make a syrup. Add boiled carrots and simmer until carrots are glazed and shiny.

COUNTRY EGGPLANT
(Berenjenas a la Paisana)

2 small eggplants
1/4 cup chopped tomatoes
1/2 cup chopped green peppers
1 teaspoon parsley

1 tablespoon olive oil
½ teaspoon
½ chopped garlic

Cut eggplants in half, lengthwise. On the cut side, make diagonal gashes and sprinkle with salt. Let stand for 30 minutes. In a frying pan, over low heat, cook the other ingredients together. In a separate frying pan bring to a boil 1/4 cup water. Place eggplants cut side up in the frying pan. Spoon sauce over and around eggplants. Cover and simmer for 20 to 25 minutes.

COUNTRY STYLE YAUTÍA "BERTY"
(Yautía Jíbara "Berty")

2 lbs. yautía (tanier)
2 teaspoons chopped garlic

1 large chopped onion
½ cup olive oil

Boil yautía in water with salt. Cook onion in olive oil until transparent. Add garlic. Drain yautía, cut in large pieces and add to the onions. Stir to coat with the olive oil and blend flavors. Add more olive oil if necessary.

GLAZED SWEET POTATOES
(Batatas Glacé)

2 lbs. sweet potatoes
1/2 cup water
3/4 cup sugar

1 teaspoon vanilla
1 tablespoon butter

Boil unpeeled sweet potatoes in salted water. Drain and peel, slice and place in oven proof glass dish. Spoon all the other ingredients over sweet potatoes and bake in 350' F oven for 30 minutes. You may also add marshmallows and unpeeled orange slices for the last 10 minutes.

EGGPLANT AU GRATIN
(Gratinado de Berenjenas)

2 medium eggplants
1 tablespoon olive oil or butter
1 medium onion- chopped
2 garlic cloves- chopped
1 teaspoon orégano
½ teaspoon salt

3 chopped tomatoes - fresh or can
1 cup grated Swiss cheese
Corn flakes crumbs
2 tablespoons Parmesan cheese
1 egg - beaten

Peel and dice eggplants. Boil for only 1 minute in about 1 inch of water with 1/2 teaspoon salt. Drain and place in a buttered oven mold. Cook onion and garlic in olive oil. Cool. Add chopped tomatoes and orégano. Spoon the mixture over the eggplant. Bake in 350' F oven for 15 minutes. Remove from oven, pour beaten egg over eggplant and sprinkle Swiss cheese, Parmesan cheese and Corn Flakes crumbs on top. Return to oven for 5 minutes or until golden.

SWEET AND SOUR STRING BEANS
(Habichuelas Tiernas en Agridulce)

1 lb. string beans
1/4 lb. bacon

3 tablespoon liquid from sweet pickles
3 tablespoons liquid from sweet pickles

Boil string beans. Drain. Chop bacon and cook in a frying pan- do not crisp. Remove bacon and grease from pan. Return about 1 tablespoon bacon grease to frying pan. Add string beans and the sweet pickles liquid. Simmer for 8 to 10 minutes.

SWEET AND SOUR BEETS
(Remolachas en Agridulce)

1/4 cup sugar
1 teaspoon cornstarch
2 tablespoons water
2 tablespoons vinegar

1 tablespoon vegetable oil
1 (16 oz) can beets
1/8 teaspoon salt

Mix sugar, cornstarch, water, vinegar, and oil. Cook over low heat until it thickens. Drain beets, add to the pan, add salt and simmer for 10 minutes.

VEGETABLE SOUFFLÉ
(Soufflé de Vegetales)

1 can Cream of Celery soup	1 onion - chopped
8 oz. frozen mixed vegetables	4 eggs
1/2 cup mayonnaise	butter
1 cup grated Cheddar cheese	Cracker Meal or Corn Flakes crumbs

Thaw and drain vegetables. Mix all ingredients together. Pour in buttered oven dish. Top with pieces of butter and Corn Flakes crumbs or Cracker Meal. Bake in 350° F oven for 45 minutes and top is brown. You may add black pepper if desired.

VEGETABLES a la GREQUE "FRAGOS"
(Vegetales a la Griega "Fragoso")

2 medium potatoes - sliced	2 green peppers – sliced
3 carrots - sliced	Cauliflower florets
1/2 lb. string beans	1 can sliced mushrooms
1 eggplant - peeled and sliced	3 sweet pickles – sliced
2 stalks celery - cut in 1 inch pieces	2 bay leaves
1 onion - sliced	**Salt to taste**

Layer all ingredients in oven proof dish. Sprinkle with salt. Pour over vegetables

1/4 cup olive oil	2 tablespoons tomato sauce
1 tablespoon vinegar	1 teaspoon Worcestershire sauce

Bake covered in 350' F oven for 30 minutes or until vegetables are tender. Remove cover and bake for 15 minutes.

GARLIC POTATOES
(Papas con Ajo)

4 Idaho potatoes	4 garlic cloves - chopped
1/4 cup butter	salt

Melt butter. Add chopped garlic. Pare and slice potatoes very thin. Place potato slices in a well buttered oven proof pan or aluminum foil, drizzle with garlic butter, sprinkle with salt and bake, covered in 350' F oven for 1 hour.

DUCHESS POTATOES
(Papas a la Duquesa)

3 lbs. potatoes - boiled	3 egg yolks
6 tablespoons butter	Milk
1/4 teaspoon nutmeg	salt

Mash potatoes until very fluffy with the milk, butter, nutmeg and salt. Beat egg yolks and mix into potatoes. Spoon into a buttered Pyrex mold. You may sprinkle with Parmesan cheese. Bake in 400' F oven until golden.

POTATO AND BACON PIE
(Pastelón de Papas y Tocineta)

1 1/2 lbs. potatoes	2 medium size onions
3 tablespoons butter	3 hard boiled eggs – sliced
1/4 cup milk	2 tablespoons Parmesan cheese
1/2 lb. sliced bacon	

Peel and boil the potatoes in salted water. Mash with the butter and milk. Fry bacon only to render some fat but do not crisp. In the same pan, with bacon grease, cook onions. Do not brown. Spread half of the mashed potatoes in buttered oven dish, top with half of the bacon slices, half of the onions and hard boiled egg slices. Top with another layer of mashed potatoes, smoothing the top with a spoon dipped in milk or butter. Top with bacon strips, onion slices and sprinkle with Parmesan cheese. Bake in 350' F oven for 30 to 40 minutes and top is brown. Garnish with sliced hard boiled eggs.

SWEET GREEN PEAS WITH HAM AND WINE
(Petit Pois con Jamón al Vino)

several slices boiled ham - chopped
1/2 can tomato sauce
1 onion - chopped
1 garlic clove - chopped

1 teaspoon parsley – chopped
1 (12 oz.) can sweet green peas
½ cup red wine

Over low heat cook ham with onion, garlic, tomato sauce and parsley. Add green peas and wine. Let mixture come to a boil, turn heat off and let stand to blend flavors. You may also add 1 bay leaf.

CORN SOUFFLÉ "MIMI"
(Soufflé de Maíz "Mimi")

1 (8 oz) can creamed corn
1 tablespoon melted butter
1 tablespoon cornstarch
1 egg – beaten

1 tablespoon sugar
Dash cinnamon
1/8 teaspoon salt

Mix all ingredients together. Pour into a well buttered baking dish and bake in 350' F oven for 45 minutes.

CORN AND CARROTS SOUFFLÉ
(Soufflé de Maíz y Zanahorias)

1 (12 oz) can diced carrots
1 (12 oz) can Corn Niblets
2 tablespoons melted butter
1 cup milk

1 tablespoon cornstarch
2 tablespoons sugar
1 beaten egg
½ teaspoon vanilla

Mix all ingredients together. Pour in a buttered oven proof pan and bake in 350' F oven for 1 hour and a cake tester emerges clean. Very good to serve with pork.

BAKED PUMPKIN
(Calabaza Asada)

2 lbs pumpkin   4 slices bacon

1 tablespoon salt

Cut Pumpkin into 4 pieces – do not peel. Remove seeds and strings. Sprinkle with salt and place a slice of bacon over each pumpkin piece. Bake at 30°F until tender.

Pastas

You can pray in any place……

RING OF PLENTY
(Aro de la Abundancia)

1 1/2 cups cooked macaroni	1 tablespoon chopped onion
1 cup grated Holland or Edam cheese	1 cup milk
1 cup cracker meal	1 egg
1 tablespoon chopped parsley	1 teaspoon salt
3 tablespoons chopped green peppers	3 tablespoons butter

Beat eggs, add all the other ingredients and pour in a buttered baking dish, Place the baking dish in a larger pan with about an inch of water. Bake in 475' F oven for 1 hour. Let stand before serving.

NEAPOLITAN FETTUCCINI
(Fettuccini Napolitano)

1 lb. fettuccini - boiled	¼ lb. butter
1 egg yolk	½ cup Parmesan cheese
2/3 cup half and half or sour cream	½ cup Parmesan Cheese
¼ lb. butter	

Beat egg yolk and add to half and half, belt butter. Drain fettuccini, add melted butter and immediately add the half and half with the egg yolk. Mix well, add Parmesan cheese and toss to mix.

ROMAN PASTA
(Pasta à la Romana)

4 oz. pasta	1 tablespoon milk
6 cups water	Salt
½ cup low fat cottage cheese	Black pepper

Cook pasta according to package directions. Mix cottage cheese with the milk and black pepper and toss with the pasta. If you are not counting calories you may add butter.

NOODLES "SAN JOSE"
(Fideos San José)

1/2 lb. thin noodles - boiled
6 eggs - separated
1/4 lb. Holland or Edam cheese
¼ lb. white cheese
½ lb. butter

Beat butter until soft, add egg yolks and beat well. Add cheeses, one at a time, beating well after each addition. Beat egg whites until very foamy and fold into cheese mixtures, then into drained noodles. Pour into well buttered glass baking dish and bake in 375' F oven until done and golden on top.

GREEN PASTA
(Pasta "Verdi")

4 oz. pasta
6 cups water
1/4 cup chopped parsley
1 cup broccoli (fresh or frozen)
2 to 3 tablespoons lime juice
1/4 cup milk or half & half
1/4 teaspoon chopped garlic
1/4 teaspoon chopped basil
1 tablespoon olive oil
1 tablespoon butter

Boil pasta in salted water for 10 minutes. Drain and toss with the butter. Boil broccoli for 3 minutes, drain and process in blender to make a paste, together with the lime juice, milk and basil. Cook garlic in olive oil. Do not brown. Add broccoli paste and simmer for 3 minutes. Add to cooked pasta and toss until well mixed.

LASAGNA WITH BACON AND CHICKEN
(Lasagna con Tocineta y Pollo)

1 box Lasagna	2 ½ teaspoons salt
3 quarts water	1 tablespoon oil

FILLING

2 1/2 lbs. chicken- remove bones and dice raw meat

1 tablespoon oil	1 onion – chopped
1/2 lb. bacon - diced	1 teaspoon garlic - chopped

2 envelopes Sazón creole seasoning with annato (available in Spanish markets)

1/2 cup white wine	½ cup Mozzarella cheese
2 bay leaves	¼ cup Cheddar cheese
1/4 cup tomato sauce	¼ cup Swiss cheese

WHITE SAUCE

4 tablespoons margarine	1 teaspoon salt
2 cups milk	2 tablespoons dry wine
4 tablespoons flour	1/8 teaspoon black pepper

Cook chicken with seasonings to make a juicy chicken stew. Make white sauce. Boil lasagna following package directions and drain. In a buttered baking pan, place a layer of lasagna, spoon filling, then sauce, cheeses, again a second layer of lasagna, again filling, sauce, and end with cheese. Cover baking dish and bake lasagna in a 400' F oven for 45 to 60 minutes. Let stand before serving.

CHICKEN LASAGNA
(Lasagna de Pollo)

Make a chicken fricasseé with 2 to 2 1/2 pounds chicken breasts. Fricasseé should be juicy. Remove skin and bones from meat. Shred meat and mix with the juice.

Add 2 hard boiled eggs - chopped
1 small can pimientos - chopped
2 tablespoons raisins
Stuffed olives – sliced
Almonds - optional
Make Bechamel Sauce below

BECHAMEL SAUCE

1 box Lasagna
4 tablespoons butter
4 tablespoons flour
2 cups milk
1 lb. Mozzarella cheese
salt
1 small onion – grated
1 small bay leaf
1 (8 oz.) can tomato sauce

Boil lasagna following package directions. While lasagna cooks, make Bechamel sauce and add the tomato sauce. Drain lasagna and place half of the lasagna strips in a large buttered oven dish. Spoon chicken meat mixture with all its juice over the lasagna. Cover with lasagna strips. Pour Bechamel sauce over the lasagna and top with the Mozzarella cheese. Bake at 375° F for 30 minutes or longer, as needed. Let stand before serving.

SPAGHETTI SAUCE
(Salsa para Spaghetti)

1 lb. ground beef
1 large onion - chopped
2 green peppers – chopped sofrito
2 bay leaves
2 teaspoons garlic - chopped
Green cilantro leaves
Long leaf culantro
Chopped parsley
2 cans Spaghetti Marinara sauce

Sauté meat together with all the ingredients, add Marinara sauce and simmer stirring occasionally for 30 to 45 minutes. Serve over boiled spaghetti and top with Parmesan cheese.

MACARONI STUFFED PEPPERS
(Pimientos Rellenos con Macarrones)

4 red or green peppers	¼ cup Cheddar cheese – diced
2 cups boiled macaroni	Tomato sauce
2 beaten eggs	Cornflake crumbs or cracker meal

Cut tops off the peppers, remove seeds and white membrane. Place pepper cases in a buttered oven dish and fill with macaroni mixed with cheese and beaten eggs. Spoon tomato sauce over the peppers and sprinkle with Corn Flakes crumbs or Cracker meal. Bake at 350' F for 30 to 40 minutes.

CAROL'S SPAGHETTI SAUCE
(Salsa "Carol" para Spaghetti)

1 lb. ground beef	1 teaspoon orégano
1 chopped onion	1 1/2 cans tomato paste
1 teaspoon salt	1 1/2 cups water
1 teaspoon sugar	Parmesan cheese

Sauté meat with chopped onion, stirring often until meat loses its pink color. Add all the other ingredients and simmer, stirring often, until sauce thickens. Serve with spaghetti and Parmesan cheese.

PASTA PRIMAVERA "LELÉ"
(Pasta Primavera "Lelé")

2/3 cup broccoli florets
1/3 cup sliced carrots
3 tablespoons olive oil
1 cup chopped mushrooms
1 tablespoon chopped onion
1/2 teaspoon chopped garlic
1/4 cup chopped green peppers
1/4 cup chopped red peppers
½ cup green peas

1 cups half & half
½ cup chopped tomatoes
½ teaspoon oregano
Salt – pepper
12 oz. fettuccini
2 tablespoons butter
4 tablespoons Parmesan

Parboil vegetables. Drain and rinse in cold water to stop cooking. In a large skillet, heat olive oil, sauté mushrooms, onion, peppers, garlic and green peas. Simmer, stirring often. Do not mash. Add 1 cup half & half and simmer until it thickens. Add all the other vegetables, tomatoes, salt, oregano and pepper. Remove from heat. Boil pasta following package directions- about 10 minutes for "al dente". Drain, rinse in cold water and return to pan. Add butter and 1 cup half & half. Mix well. Heat the vegetable mixture and add to the pasta. Toss with the Parmesan cheese and chopped basil. You can also add chopped parsley.

MACARONI SOUFFLÉ
(Soufflé de Macarrones)

1 cup boiled macaroni
1 can Corned Beef or
boiled beef sautéed with chopped onions
1 lb. tomatoes - peeled and chopped
3 oz . cream cheese

1 cup milk
¼ teaspoon cornstarch

1 tablespoon cornstarch
1 tablespoon butter

Chop boiled macaroni. Mix milk with all the other ingredients. Add to macaroni and mix well. Pour in buttered oven dish and bake at 350' F for 45 minutes. You may sprinkle top with Corn Flakes crumbs and Parmesan cheese before baking.

MACARONI TIMBALE
(Timbal de Macarrones)

1 cup macaroni or spaghetti	¼ teaspoon nutmeg
4 tablespoons Cracker meal	1 tablespoon chopped onion
1/4 lb. butter	¼ cup
1/4 lb. Holland or Edam cheese – grated	

Boil macaroni. Rinse in cold water and chop in small pieces. Heat milk and butter. Add all the other ingredients, mixing well together. Pour in a well buttered baking dish. Bake at 350°F until top is brown.

SPAGHETTI CARBONARA "JULY"
(Spaghetti Carbonara "July")

1 box spaghetti # 8	
1/4 lb. sliced bacon	2 tablespoons olive oil
1/2 teaspoon chopped garlic	2 tablespoons butter
1/2 lb. boiled ham -cut in strips	3/4 cup chopped parsley
1/3 cup Parmesan cheese	salt - pepper
1/4 cup black olives	3 beaten eggs
1 envelope Sazón creole seasoning	2 pimientos - sliced

Fry bacon crisp. Chop. Discard fat. In same skillet, add oil butter, garlic and ham. Cook for 10 minutes. Mix in spaghetti, butter, cheese, parsley, Sazón ,salt and pepper to taste. Remove from heat, add eggs, stir. Return to low heat, stirring often. Add olives and pimiento strips.

Sauces

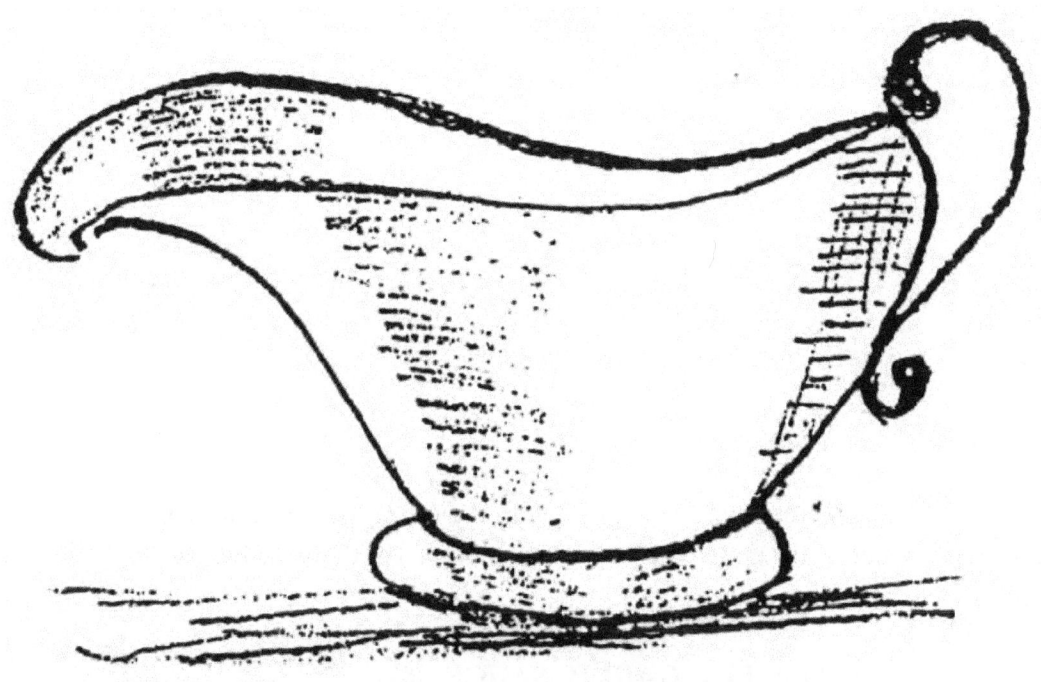

Give me Oh Lord,
the humility to learn from my
child while I am teaching him...

AVOCADO DRESSING OR GUACAMOLE
(Aderezo de Aguacate o Guacamole)

1 ripe avocado	1 onion – chopped
2 tablespoons lime juice or vinegar	1 tomato – chopped
1 teaspoon chopped garlic	½ cup olive oil
1 teaspoon salt	green cilantro leaves - chopped

Mash avocado with a fork, immediately add lime juice or vinegar to prevent fruit from darkening. Add olive oil and all the other ingredients. Correct seasoning. If the dressing is too thick, add more olive oil and lime juice.

AJILIMÓJILI
(Ajilimójili)

6 tomatoes	fresh cilantro leaves
2 large onions	long leaf culantro
1 green pepper	lime juice or white vinegar
1 red pepper	olive oil
10 sweet red chiles	salt

Chop all ingredients in very small pieces and mix with the salt, lime juice, and olive oil. You may add chopped avocado. If you add avocado, do so at the very last and toss gently.

AIOLI OR GARLIC SAUCE
(Aioli o Salsa de Ajo)

4 cloves garlic - chopped	1 slice white bread – crust removed and cubed
2 egg yolks	½ teaspoon ice water
1/8 teaspoon salt	1 teaspoon lime juice

Beat egg yolks, chopped garlic, salt and white bread until well mixed. Add olive oil very slowly, beating continuously. As sauce thickens add 1/2 teaspoon ice water and lime juice, beating constantly. You may add chopped parsley. This sauce can also be made without the egg yolks but it will not be as flavorful. Very good with fish.

BUTTER SAUCE
(Salsa de Mantequilla)

2 eggs
2 tablespoons lime juice
¼ teaspoon salt
1 cup (1/2 lb.) butter

In blender beat 2 eggs, lime juice and salt. Melt butter and while still hot, add very slowly to beaten eggs, beating constantly, until well blended. Let stand before serving. Add nutmeg or parsley if desired. (Makes 1 -2/3 cups)

GARLIC MAYONNAISE
(Mayonesa de Ajo)

3 cloves garlic - chopped
2 egg yolks
1/2 cup olive oil
1 teaspoon lime juice or vinegar
Salt
White pepper

In the blender or with a wire whisk, beat egg yolks and garlic. Very slowly and beating continuously, add the olive oil, in a thin stream, until it thickens. Add lime juice or vinegar, salt and pepper. Beat well and refrigerate.

VINAIGRETTE SAUCE *(For Lobster or Fish)*
(Salsa Vinagreta (Para Langosta o Pescado))

4 hard boiled eggs
1 cup olive oil
salt - black pepper

1/2 cup vinegar
1 large onion – chopped
1 can pimentos – chopped
18 – 20 pimento stuffed olives – sliced
Parsley - chopped

Separate egg yolks and egg whites. Mash yolks and add olive oil, beating to make a paste. Add vinegar, stirring constantly. Add vinegar and mix well. Chop egg whites and add, along with chopped onion, parsley, pimientos, olives, salt and pepper. Mix well, correct seasoning. Serve over boiled lobster or fish.

BECHAMEL SAUCE
(Salsa Bechamel)

4 tablespoons butter	½ teaspoon salt
1/2 cup flour	White pepper
4 cups hot milk	Nutmeg

Melt butter. Add flour all at once, stirring constantly with an egg turner or a wire whisk. Do not let the flour turn brown. Add the hot milk all at once and beat vigorously to prevent lumping. Continue cooking over very low heat stirring constantly until thickened and creamy. Add seasonings.

Variations:
You may add 2 tablespoons chopped onions sautéed in the butter before adding the flour. Or you can boil the milk with a sprig of parsley.

BECHAMEL SAUCE WITH EGG
(Salsa Bechamel con Huevo)

2 tablespoons butter	¼ teaspoon ground nutmeg
2 tablespoons flour or cornstarch	½ bay leaf
salt	1 tablespoon
ground pepper	2 beaten egg yolks
1 cup hot milk	

Melt butter over very low heat, add flour or cornstarch, all at once, stirring constantly for a while. Do not brown. Add hot milk and seasonings and cook until thickened. Remove from heat and add some of the sauce to the beaten egg yolks, mixing well. Add to the hot sauce and beat to mix well.

MAÎTRE D'HÔTEL SAUCE
(Salsa Maître D'Hotel)

4 tablespoons butter
2 teaspoons chopped parsley
1 teaspoon ground nutmeg
4 tablespoons lime juice
½ teaspoon salt

Mix all ingredients together. Serve over roast meat or with vegetables.

SAUCE FOR VEGETABLES
(Salsa para Vegetales)

2 tablespoons chopped onions
2 tablespoons butter
1 can Cream of Chicken soup
1/3 cup milk
3 tablespoons chopped parsley
2 tablespoons lime juice
1 tablespoon Sherry wine (optional)

Put all ingredients together in a sauce pan and simmer over low heat. Serve with vegetables.

ANCHOVY VINAIGRETTE
(Vinagreta de Anchoas)

2 anchovy fillets - mashed
1/2 teaspoon salt
ground black pepper (optional)
½ cup olive oil
2 tablespoon wine

Beat all ingredients together until creamy. You can also add Dijon mustard or lime juice.

Fritters

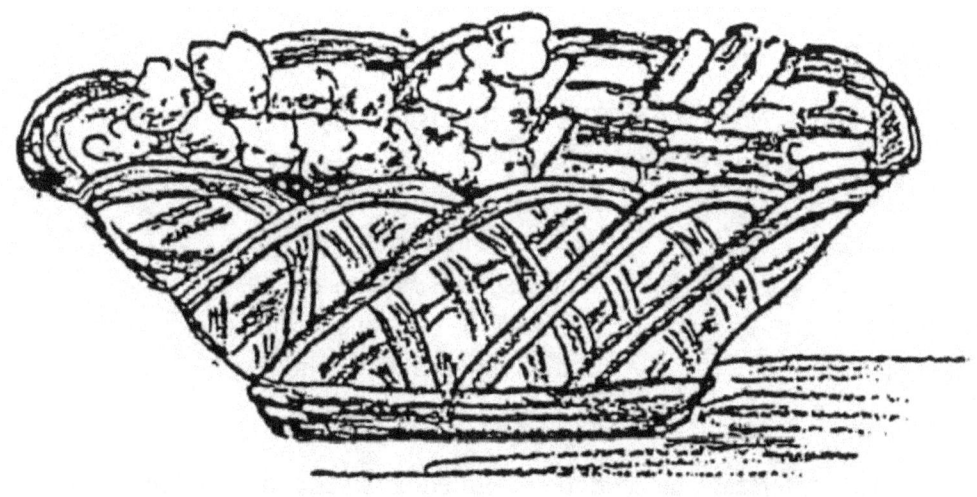

There is always a ray of
sunlight shining through
every cloud.....

RICE MEAL FRITTERS "DOÑA ANA"
(Almojábanas "doña Ana")

1 lb. rice meal
1 teaspoon salt
1 teaspoon sugar
1 teaspoon baking powder

4 tablespoons milk
1 tablespoon melted butter
1 lb. white country cheese – grated
4 large eggs

Beat eggs, add all ingredients except the cheese. After all ingredients are well mixed, add the cheese and stir to mix. Refrigerate, covered, overnight. Shape into walnut-size balls, or drop from a teaspoon into hot fat, turning often until cooked and browned.

RICE MEAL FRITTERS "ISABEL"
(Almojábanas "Isabel")

2 cups rice meal
2 tablespoons flour
1 teaspoon salt
1 teaspoon baking powder
4 to 5 eggs

1/2 lb. white country cheese
2 tablespoons Parmesan cheese
1 (14 1/2 oz) can evaporated milk
1 stick margarine - melted

Mix dry ingredients together. Beat eggs, add to dry ingredients. Add milk and melted margarine. With a fork, mash the white cheese and add to the batter, together with the Parmesan cheese. Refrigerate overnight. It keeps well in the refrigerator and improves its flavor after several days. Drop batter from a teaspoon into deep hot fat, stirring often until golden brown.

YAUTÍA FRITTERS
(Frituras de Yautía)

2 lbs. yautía (tanier)
1 1/2 teaspoon salt

1 teaspoon baking powder
1 chopped garlic clove

Peel and grate yautía. Mix all ingredients together and drop from a teaspoon into deep hot fat, stirring often until cooked and golden.

CORN MEAL FRITTERS
(Buñuelos de Harina de Maíz)

1 cup flour
1 cup corn meal
2 eggs
1 teaspoon salt
1/4 cup water

1/2 cup milk
2 teaspoons margarine - melted
1/2 teaspoon baking powder
1/2 cup grated Cheddar cheese

Mix dry ingredients together. Add eggs one at a time, beating continuously. Add butter, then water and milk, beating to form a soft batter. Let stand for 1/2 hour. When ready to fry add grated cheese. Drop into hot fat a teaspoon at a time and fry until golden brown.

SAN GERMÁN'S CODFISH FRITTERS
(Bacalaítos Sangermeños)

1 lb. salt codfish
2 green peppers
1 onions
7 garlic cloves

3 to 4 sweet chiles
2 cups self-rising flour
2 cups water
sprig of cilantro

In water to cover, soak codfish overnight. Discard skin and bones. Chop codfish in blender or in meat grinder, adding water from the 2 cups in the recipe. Remove to a bowl. Grind the onions, green peppers, garlic, chiles and cilantro. Add to the codfish together with the flour and reserved water. You may also add annato oil for coloring and pepper to taste. Drop from a teaspoon into deep hot fat-, stirring and turning until golden.

GRAINS OF RICE FROM THE EAST
(Granitos de Arroz del Este)

1 lb. rice meal
3 cups water

½ teaspoon salt
¼ lb. Cheddar cheese, diced

Cook the rice meal in salted water, stirring continuously to keep from sticking to the pan, until it forms a stiff dough. Remove from stove and pour on a platter to cool. Shape into walnut-size balls and push a piece of the cheese into each ball. Fry in deep hot fat, turning often until golden.

CORN MEAL STICKS WITH COCONUT
(Surullitos de Maíz con Coco)

4 cups fresh coconut milk	1 tablespoon sugar
2 1/2 cups corn meal	1 teaspoon salt or to taste

Mix all ingredients together and cook over very low heat, stirring constantly until very thick and the dough separates from the sides of the pan. Turn on a platter. When cool enough to handle, knead until smooth and shape into finger- size sticks. Drop in hot fat and fry until golden.

OLD WOMAN'S BELLIES "MINILLAS"
(Barrigas de Vieja "Minillas")

1 lb. pumpkin	2 tablespoons sugar
1 teaspoon salt	1/2 cup flour
1 tablespoon melted margarine	1/4 teaspoon cinnamon
1 egg	½ teaspoon vanilla

Boil unpeeled pumpkin in salted water. Scrape the pulp from the shell to measure about 1 cup pumpkin. Add all the other ingredients and mix well. Adjust seasonings. Drop from a teaspoon into hot fat. When brown on one side, turn to brown the other side. Drain on paper towels. The pumpkin used in these recipes is the creole pumpkin. Do not use squash or Thanksgiving pumpkin.

DOUGHNUTS "POLY"
(Donas "Poly")

2 beaten eggs	2 cups self-rising flour
½ cup sugar	½ cup sugar
½ teaspoon vanilla	2 teaspoons melted butter

Beat eggs with sugar and vanilla. Add flour, nutmeg and margarine. Mix well but do not overbeat. Drop from a teaspoon into hot oil and fry until golden. Drain and sprinkle with sugar. You may also add cinnamon to the sugar.

GARBANZO FRITTERS
(Frituras de Garbanzos)

1 lb. garbanzo beans - boiled or 1 can garbanzos   1/2 teaspoon salt
2 tablespoons flour   1 beaten egg

Drain well and mash the garbanzos. Add flour, salt and beaten egg, mixing well. Shape into patties and fry in shallow fat.

CREAMED CORN FRITTERS
(Frituras de Maíz a la Crema)

1 (8 oz) can creamed corn   1 ½ cups flour
1 egg   1 teaspoon baking powder
2 heaping tablespoons sugar   salt

Mix all ingredients together. Fry in hot fat, dropping from a teaspoon. Turn when brown on one side and brown the other side. Drain on paper towels and serve or dust with Confectioners' sugar.

ÑAME FRITTERS "LELÉ"
(Buñuelos de Ñame "Lelé")

1 lb. ñame (yam)   2 beaten eggs
3 tablespoons flour   1 ½ teaspoons salt

Mix all ingredients together. Drop batter from a teaspoon into hot fat. Drain on paper towels and serve while still warm. You can also serve these fritters with a syrup made with 2 cups sugar, 1 cup water and 1 stick cinnamon. After well drained, place fritters in a bowl and pour cool syrup over them.

MAMA CELIA'S DOUGHNUTS
(Donas Mamá Celia)

2 cups flour	1 egg
1/2 cup sugar	1 ½ teaspoons butter
1 teaspoon cinnamon	½ cup milk
1/8 teaspoon nutmeg	½ tablespoon lime juice
½ teaspoon salt	Sugar

Mix lime juice and milk to curdle. Mix all ingredients except sugar together, stirring with a wooden spoon. Cover and refrigerate for 2 hours or overnight. Knead, using flour sparingly. Pat or roll dough, about 1 inch thick and cut with a doughnut cutter. Fry in deep hot fat until golden, turning often.

Drain and sprinkle with sugar.

Rice and Grains

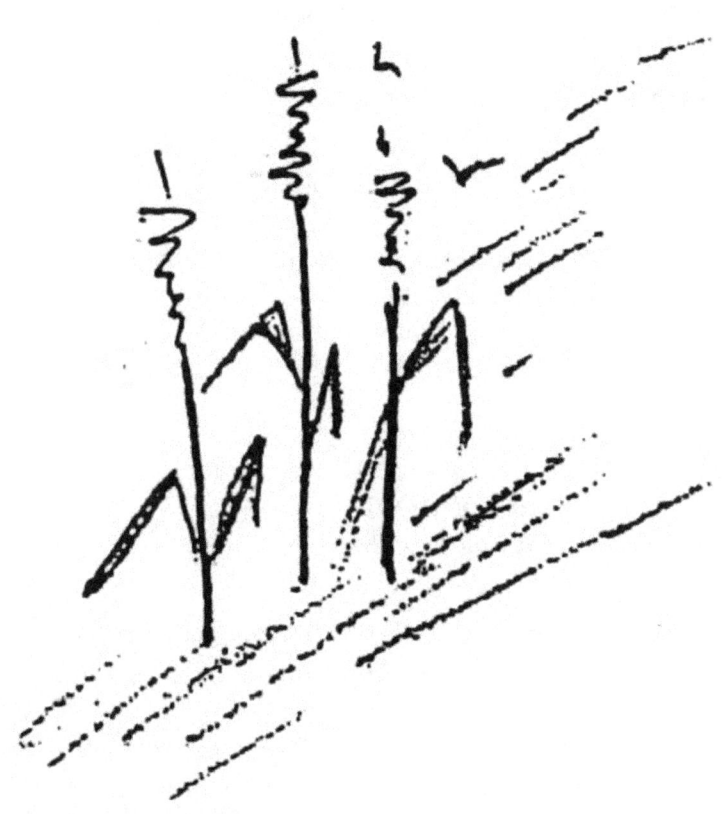

Autumn is
the best season of life because
in it one finds beauty and peace....

CHICKEN AND RICE WITH BEER
(Arroz can Pollo y Cerveza)

1 (2 1/2 to 3 lb) chicken	1/2 teaspoon orégano
2 tablespoons sofrito	1 tablespoon salt
2 oz. cooking ham	1/2 teaspoon black pepper
2 oz. salt pork fat	2 bay leaves
4 tablespoons tomato sauce	3 cups rice
1 tablespoon annato oil	2 cans beer
3 tablespoons vegetable oil	capers - olives

Sauté salt pork and cooking ham. Add sofrito, bay leaves and tomato sauce. Add chicken, stir, cover and cook for 30 minutes over low heat. Add rice, capers, olives and beer. Mix well. Cook uncovered, until liquid is absorbed. Lower heat, turn rice and cover until done. Garnish with pimientos, small green peas, asparagus tips.

RICE RING
(Corona de Arroz)

2 cups cooked rice	1/2 cup chopped green peppers
1/2 cup chopped tomatoes	1/2 cup Holland or Edam cheese

Mix all ingredients together and pour in well buttered oven dish. You may sprinkle more cheese over rice, if desired. Bake in 350' F oven for 20 minutes. Let rest and unmold.

FRIED NAVY BEANS
(Habichuelas Blancas Fritas)

2 cups boiled white beans - cold and drained
1/2 stick margarine   1 tablespoon olive oil

Beans should be well drained and cold. Heat margarine and olive oil in a skillet or frying pan, add beans. Stir constantly over high heat until the beans are golden and crisp on the outside. You may substitute with boiled garbanzos, adding crisp bacon or Spanish chorizos.

RICE AND PICKLED FISH "SAN LUIS"
(Arroz con Escabeche "San Luis ")

3 pieces pickled fish (escabeche)	1 large onion – chopped
2 cups rice	3 cups water
3 tablespoons oil from pickled fish	Salt to taste
1 tablespoon sofrito	Peppercorns
1/2 cup tomato sauce	Olives
1 bay leaf	

Sauté sofrito in oil from pickled fish, add onions, tomato sauce, bay leaf, olives and peppercorns. Add water, (about 3 cups), salt and rice. Cook, uncovered, until liquid is absorbed. Turn rice, cover, and cook until done. Garnish with canned pimientos and green peas.

RICE WITH ASPARAGUS
(Arroz con Espárragos)

1 can asparagus tips	1 ½ cups rice
4 tablespoons butter	2 cups chicken or beef consommé
1 large onion - chopped	4 tablespoons Parmesan Cheese

Cook onion in butter over low heat, add liquid from asparagus and consommé. Let come to a boil and add rice. Cook uncovered until liquid is absorbed. Add asparagus, saving several tips for garnish. Add more butter if needed and Parmesan cheese. Turn rice gently. Cover and cook until done. You may use Brussel sprouts instead of asparagus if desired.

RICE "ALHAMBRA"
(Arroz "La Alhambra")

BECHAMEL SAUCE

2 cups cooked rice	8 tablespoons butter
2 cups Parmesan cheese	8 tablespoons flour
8 eggs - separated	2 cups milk
	¼ teaspoon salt

Beat egg yolks, toss rice with the yolks and the Parmesan cheese. Make Bechamel sauce. Add sauce to rice and mix well. Beat egg whites until stiff and fold into rice mixture. Pour in a buttered oven dish and bake at 350°F until a tester emerges clean and the top is brown.

RICE WITH CABBAGE
(Arroz con Repollo)

1 cup shredded cabbage	4 tablespoons butter
2 cups rice	2 tablespoons sofrito
4 cups chicken consommé	

Cook shredded cabbage in butter until wilted. Remove cabbage to a bowl. Add olive oil or butter to pan, stir in sofrito, then rice, and stir well to cover rice with sofrito. Add hot consommé. Cook, uncovered, until liquid is absorbed but rice is still moist. Add cabbage, stir, cover, and cook until done. You may add Parmesan cheese if you wish.

LIMA BEANS WITH SPANISH SAUSAGES
(Habas con Chorizos)

1 can Lima beans	1 tablespoon catsup
1/4 cup sofrito	1 to 2 chorizos

Sauté chorizos, add catsup and Lima beans, mix and cook over low heat for 20 to 30 minutes, stirring often very gently.

STUFFED RICE
(Arroz Relleno)

2 1/2 lbs. rice	2 tablespoons olive oil
1/4 lb. Parmesan cheese	Sofrito
1/2 lb. Holland or Edam cheese - sliced	Tomato sauce
2 1/2 to 3 lbs. chicken parts	Canned pimentos

Make a chicken fricassée. It should be juicy. Discard skin and bones. Mix meat with about half of the fricassée sauce. Cook rice with olive oil, sofrito, tomato sauce and the reserved fricassée sauce. Add water if necessary and cook rice until done. In a buttered oven dish layer rice, alternating with the chicken meat, sauce and cheese. The last layer should be rice and then cheese. Bake at 350°F for 20 to 30 minutes. Garnish with pimientos, asparagus, peas, etc...

GARBANZO CASSEROLE "IRMA"
(Cacerola de Garbanzos "Irma")

2 cans boiled garbanzos - drained	**Sauce**
2 lbs. potatoes - boiled	2 cans tomato sauce
1 lb. cabbage - parboiled	1/2 cup olive oil
1 can chorizo (4 or 5 chorizos)	1/4 cup vinegar
1 (6 oz) can pimientos	
1 lb. bacon - sliced	

In an oven proof casserole dish, layer ingredients. Top with sliced bacon. In a separate bowl mix sauce ingredients and pour over garbanzos. Bake at 350°F for 50 minutes or longer.

RICE WITH OKRA
(Arroz con Guingambó)

1 onion - chopped	1 teaspoon vinegar
1/2 lb. okra - sliced	2 cups rice
3 tablespoons olive oil	1 1/2 cups hot water
4 tablespoons tomato sauce	2 teaspoons salt

Cook onion in olive oil, add sliced okra, stirring well. Add tomato sauce and vinegar, mixing well. Add rice, hot water and salt, and let come to a boil. When part of the liquid has been absorbed, turn rice, cover and cook until done, turning rice once or twice.

RICE WITH VIENNA SAUSAGES AND RED WINE
(Arroz con Salchichas y Vino Tinto)

1/2 cup olive oil	2 1/2 cups rice
2 garlic cloves	2 cups water
1 onion - chopped	1/4 cup red wine
sofrito	2 cans Vienna sausages
1/2 cup tomato sauce	6 tablespoons Parmesan cheese

Cook garlic, onion, sofrito and tomato sauce in olive oil. Mix in rice and Vienna sausages, stirring to coat rice with sofrito. Add water and wine. Let boil gently until liquid is absorbed. Turn rice, cover pot and cook over low heat until done. Sprinkle Parmesan cheese over rice. Garnish with pimiento slices. (Sofrito - see Index)

RICE "SANTA ROSA"
(Arroz "Santa Rosa")

3 tablespoons olive oil	1 can sliced mushrooms
1 cup chopped onions	2 green peppers – chopped
1 tomato - skinned and chopped	1 teaspoon salt
1 lb. eggplants - peeled and cubed	2 cups boiled rice

Sauté vegetables with the olive oil, then simmer for 10 minutes. Add boiled rice, stir well and let stand for several minutes before serving. Sprinkle top with Parmesan cheese, if desired, and broil to brown top.

BEANS IN SALSA MOJO
(Habichuelas en Mojo)

1 lb. Kidney beans	1 tablespoon Paprika
4 large onions - sliced	1 bay leaf
1 can tomato sauce	1 teaspoon peppercorns
1 cup olive oil	sofrito
1 cup vinegar	salt
3 green peppers - chopped	

You may use 2 cans boiled Kidney beans instead of boiling your own. Drain boiled Kidney beans and mix with all the other ingredients. Simmer until sauce thickens.

BLACK BEANS
(Habichuelas Negras)

1 lb. black beans
3 cups water
1 green pepper
1 onion
2 sweet chiles

1 teaspoon chopped garlic
1/2 cup olive oil
1 cup red wine
salt

Soak beans, overnight, in 3 cups water. In the same water, over low heat, boil beans with green pepper, onion, sweet chiles and garlic. When beans are tender, add olive oil, wine and salt to taste, and cook until sauce thickens.

PICKLED PIGEON PEAS "QUIQUE"
(Gandules en Escabeche "Quique")

2 lbs. pigeon peas - boiled
3 small onions - chopped
2 green peppers - chopped
2 leaves long leaf culantro - chopped
1 cup olive oil

½ cup vinegar
Tabasco sauce
Worcestershire sauce
Garlic – minced
salt

Drain pigeon peas. Mix well with all the other ingredients. Let stand for several hours or overnight before serving. Refrigerate.

NAVY BEANS WITH CODFISH "a la YAUREL"
(Habichuelas con Bacalao "a la Yaurel")

1 lb. salt codfish - boiled and flaked	1 lb. potatoes – parboiled and sliced
1 lb. tomatoes - peeled and chopped	2 onions – sliced
1 can pimientos	2 tablespoons olive oil
2 teaspoons garlic - chopped	2 tablespoons vinegar
1 lb. Navy beans - boiled and drained	

Over low heat cook the tomatoes in olive oil with garlic and vinegar to make a sauce. Layer all ingredients in an oven proof pan and top with the tomato sauce. Bake for 60 minutes at 350°F. Garnish with pimiento strips and parsley.

BAKED RICE WITH PORK CHOPS
(Arroz con Chuletas al Horno)

1/2 stick margarine	4 cups water
1/2 cup chopped onions	1 green pepper - sliced
1/2 cup chopped green peppers	1/2 onion - sliced
3 cups long grain rice	1 tomato - sliced
2 envelopes dehydrated onion soup	6 pork chops

Season chops. Cook chopped onions in margarine, add water and dehydrated onion soup. Let water come to a boil, add rice and boil until liquid is absorbed. Spoon rice into an oven proof rectangular dish. Brown pork chops and place on top of the rice. Top each pork chop with 1 tomato slice, 1 onion slice and 1 green pepper slice. Cover pan with aluminum foil and bake at 350' until cooked. You may substitute with chicken.

GOOD FRIDAY RICE
(Arroz Viernes Santo)

¼ lb. butter
1/2 cup chopped onions
3 1/2 cups water
4 cubes chicken consommé
1 teaspoon salt

1 teaspoon saffron
2 1/2 cups rice
1/2 cup Parmesan cheese
2 eggs

Cook onion with about 1 tablespoon margarine. Add saffron, salt, water, and chicken consommé cubes. Let water come to a boil, add rice, stir and cook, uncovered, until liquid is absorbed. Turn to low heat and cover pot. Beat the 2 eggs, season with salt and fry to make thin omelets. Cut omelets in strips and add to the rice. Stir, cover and cook until done. When ready to serve add the reserved margarine and Parmesan cheese. Garnish with pimientos, asparagus and green peas.

FRIED GARBANZOS "MAMÁ"
(Garbanzos Fritos de Mamá)

2 cans boiled garbanzos – drained
6 slices of bacon – cut in pieces

1 chopped onion
¼ teaspoon salt

Fry bacon. Do not crisp. Add onion and cook until onion is transparent. Do not brown onion. Add well drained garbanzos, toss to cover with bacon grease and cook until golden

Breads

Give us this day,
our daily bread....

COFFEE RING
(Anillo de Pan para Café)

2 1/2 cups flour	1/2 stick butter - melted
2 1/2 teaspoons baking powder	1 egg - beaten
1 teaspoon salt	1/3 cup brown sugar
4 tablespoons sugar	1/2 cup chopped walnuts
3 tablespoons butter	1/2 cup raisins
2 tablespoons Crisco	1 teaspoon ground cinnamon
7 tablespoons milk	1 teaspoon grated lemon peel

Glaze:
1 cup Confectioners' sugar
2 tablespoons milk or 2 tablespoons lemon juice

Sift flour before measuring. Sift together flour, salt, baking powder and 4 tablespoons sugar. Cut in Crisco and butter. In a separate bowl stir together egg and milk, and mix into flour mixture to form a ball. Knead for 1 minute on a lightly floured board and roll to form a rectangle inch thick. Brush dough with the melted butter. In a bowl mix the brown sugar, cinnamon, walnuts, raisins and grated lemon peel. Pour this mixture forming a line in the center of the rectangle and roll as for a jelly roll, bringing the ends together to form a circle, pinching the two ends to make them hold. Make perpendicular cuts on top of the ring, about 2 inches apart. Place in a buttered baking sheet. Bake at 375°F for 25 to 35 minutes. Remove from oven and glaze.

SWEET POTATO BREAD
(Pan de Batata)

2 lbs. sweet potatoes	1/8 teaspoon ground cloves
2 eggs	2/3 cup brown sugar - packed
1/2 stick butter	1/4 cup orange juice
2 cups flour	1 tablespoon grated orange peel
2 teaspoons baking powder	1/3 cup raisins
1 teaspoon nutmeg	1/3 cup walnuts - chopped
1/4 teaspoon allspice	1 teaspoon baking soda
1 teaspoon salt	

Measure 1 cup mashed sweet potatoes. Let stand until cool. Beat eggs and melted butter together. Add mashed sweet potatoes, brown sugar, orange juice and orange peel, beating to mix well. Sift dry ingredients together and mix into sweet potatoes. Add walnuts and raisins. Mix well. Pour batter into a well buttered loaf pan. Bake at 350°F for lb minutes or until cake tester emerges clean.

SWEET POTATO AND COFFEE BREAD
(Pan de Batata con Cafe)

1/4 cup butter - melted	1 teaspoon salt
1/2 cup vegetable oil	1 teaspoon cinnamon
2 2/3 cups sugar	1 1/2 teaspoons nutmeg
4 eggs	2 teaspoons baking soda
2 cups mashed sweet potatoes	1 cup chopped walnuts
3 1/2 cups sifted flour	2/3 cup coffee

Boil 3 lbs. sweet potatoes and mash to measure 2 cups. Beat together butter, vegetable oil and sugar. Add eggs one at a time, beating well after each addition. Add sweet potatoes. Mix well. Sift dry ingredients together. If using chopped walnuts (optional), mix now into the dry ingredients, then add dry ingredients to the sweet potato mixture and mix well. Bake in two buttered 4 1/2 x 8 pan for 60 minutes at 350' F. Test for doneness. Cool for 15 minutes before unmolding. (You may substitute orange juice for the coffee and use raisins instead of walnuts.)

JALAPEÑO CORNBREAD….. (HOT!!!)
(Pan de Maíz con Chile Jalapeño…. (Picante!!!)

1 can creamed corn	1 (3 1/3 oz) can chili peppers
1 cup corn meal	1 teaspoon salt
1 cup grated Cheddar cheese	1/2 teaspoon baking soda
3/4 cup milk	2 tablespoons butter
3 beaten eggs	

Mix creamed corn and corn meal, about half the Cheddar cheese, milk, eggs, chopped chili peppers, salt and baking soda. Put butter in a heavy in a heavy clay or iron mold, and heat in a 400' F oven until butter is melted. Pour batter into hot mold, sprinkle Cheddar cheese on top, and bake at 400'F. for 40 to 45 minutes. Test for doneness. If it browns too rapidly, cover with aluminum foil and leave in the oven until a cake tester emerges clean.

CORN BREAD "TAI"
(Pan de Maíz con "Tai")

1/4 cup butter	4 teaspoons baking powder
1 1/2 cups sugar	1 teaspoon salt
1 1/4 cups flour	1 1/3 cups fresh coconut milk
1 1/4 cups corn meal	3 egg whites

Sift dry ingredients together. Beat butter, add sugar, a tablespoon at a time, beating until very creamy. Add dry ingredients, alternately with the coconut milk. Mix well. Beat egg whites until stiff and fold into the other mixture. Pour in a well buttered shallow cake pan. Bake at 350°F for 30 to 35 minutes or until done and golden. Do not unmold.

CINNAMON RAISIN ROLLS "CARMELA"
(Panecillos de Canela y Pasas "Carmela")

2 cups flour	1 teaspoon salt
2/3 cup cold milk	2 tablespoons melted margarine
5 oz. Crisco	1/4 cup brown sugar - packed
3 teaspoons baking powder	1 teaspoon cinnamon
1/4 cup raisins	

Sift flour, measure and sift together with salt and baking powder. Cut in Crisco. Add cold milk slowly, mixing with a fork until dough forms a ball. Knead on a lightly floured board, roll into a rectangle 18 inches long. Brush with melted margarine. Mix together raisins, cinnamon and brown sugar. Spread mixture over dough and roll jelly roll fashion. Moisten edges with water and press together to seal. Cut into 1 1/2 inch slices. Place in a buttered pan. Bake at 325°F for 15 minutes or until done and golden.

WALNUT BREAD
(Pan de Nueces)

2 1/2 cups flour	1 cup milk
1/2 cup sugar	4 teaspoons baking powder
1 egg	1 cup chopped walnuts
1/2 teaspoon salt	

Beat all ingredients together until smooth. Pour in a well buttered 4 1/2 × 8 mold. Let stand 20 minutes. Bake at 350°F for 40 minutes. Test for doneness.

BANANA BREAD
(Pan de Guineo)

¾ stick butter	½ cup milk
¾ cup sugar	2 cups flour
1 egg	2 teaspoons baking powder
1 tablespoon grated lemon peel	¼ teaspoon salt
1 teaspoon vanilla	3 sliced ripe bananas

Sift dry ingredients together. Beat butter and sugar, add egg, grated lemon peel, vanilla and milk until creamy. Add sifted dry ingredients and beat well. Fold in sliced bananas. Pour batter in a buttered loaf pan and top with the **Streusel topping**.

STREUSEL TOPPING

1/3 cup flour	¾ teaspoons ground cinnamon
1/3 cup Brown sugar – packed	4 tablespoons butter

With two knives, cut ingredients together and spoon over the batter. Bake in 375°F oven for 45 minutes.

CORN BREAD "TIA DELIA"
(Pan de Maíz "Tía Delia")

1 1/2 cups corn meal	2 tablespoons butter
1 cup milk	1/2 teaspoon ground cinnamon
1 cup fresh coconut milk	1/2 teaspoon salt
4 eggs	1 teaspoon baking powder
1 1/4 cups sugar	

Sift together flour, salt, cinnamon and baking powder. Beat eggs and sugar until creamy. Add butter and mix well. Add the sifted ingredients alternating with the coconut milk and beat until blended. Pour in a buttered rectangular pan and bake at 300'F. for 1 hour. Test for doneness.

MILKLESS CORN BREAD
(Pan de Maíz sin Leche)

1 cup flour	1/2 teaspoon salt
1 cup corn meal	2 eggs
2 tablespoons sugar	1/4 cup vegetable oil
4 teaspoons baking powder use	One of the milk substitutes listed below

Select one of the following milk substitutes:
- 1 cup pear nectar
- 1 cup apple juice
- 1/3 cup peanut butter + apple juice to measure 1 cup
- 1/4 cup chopped carrots + soy milk to measure 1 cup

Mix dry ingredients together. Add eggs, your choice from 1-2-3-4- and vegetable oil. Stir until mixed. Do not over beat. Bake in a buttered cake pan at 425' for 20 to 25 minutes.

BREAD.....ONLY BREAD
(Pan……Pan)

2 cups flour	1 cup sugar
2 1/2 teaspoons baking powder	2 eggs
1/2 tablespoon salt	8 tablespoons milk
3 oz. butter	

TOPPING

3 tablespoons Confectioners' sugar	2 oz. butter
6 tablespoons flour	½ cup chopped nuts
1/2 teaspoon cinnamon	¼ teaspoon almond extract
1/4 teaspoon salt	

Sift dry ingredients together. Beat butter and sugar until creamy. Add eggs one at a time, beating well after each addition. Slowly add dry ingredients, alternating with milk. Pour in well buttered S inch pans. Mix topping ingredients together, spread over batter and bake at 350* for 30 minutes.

Desserts and Candies

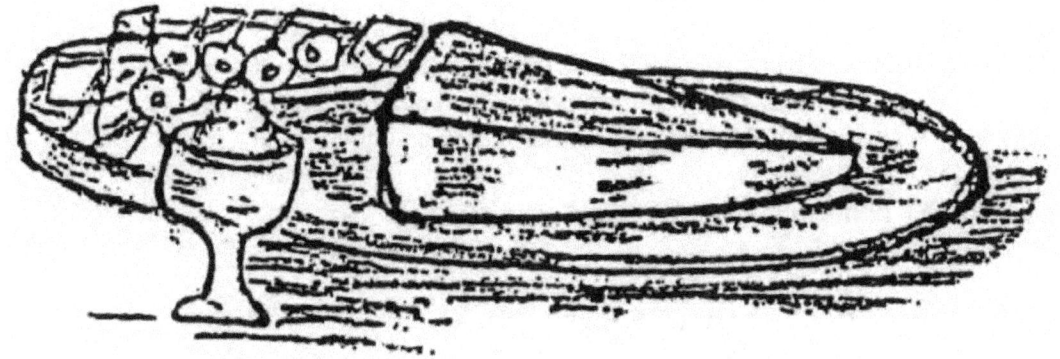

Blessings come
in different forms....

SWEET RICE AND COCONUT "BEBA"
(Arroz con Dulce "Beba")

1 ½ cups rice   3 cups water
6 to 8 prunes

In a heavy iron or aluminum pot, in 3 cups water, boil the rice with the prunes. Meanwhile, measure the following ingredients in a bowl:

1 1/2 cups sugar	1 ½ teaspoons ground cloves
1 1/2 teaspoons salt	3 tablespoons Brandy
1 1/2 teaspoons ground ginger	1 ½ tablespoons butter
1 1/2 teaspoons ground cinnamon	1 small box raisins
1 1/2 teaspoons ground cloves	3 cups fresh coconut milk

When the water in the rice is partially absorbed, add all the dry ingredients to the rice. Stir, lower the heat and cover the pot, stirring occasionally until all the liquid is absorbed. Pour on a platter and let stand. Sometimes oil will accumulate on top of the rice. Absorb it with a paper towel. You may sprinkle Parmesan cheese over the rice. Garnish with whole prunes, walnuts, figs, cherries. Note; Never add sugar before the rice is cooked. Sugar will not allow the rice to get tender.

HEAVENLY BREAD PUDDING
(Budín del Cielo)

1 lb. sandwich bread	4 egg yolks
1 quart milk	1 cup sugar
1/2 lb. Danish butter	1 teaspoon vanilla
4 whole eggs	1 guava paste – cut in strips

MERINGUE

4 egg whites   4 tablespoons sugar

Whirl together in a blender or put through a sieve all the ingredients except the guava paste. Bake in a well buttered baking dish for 1 hour at 350°F. Remove from oven and immediately push strips of guava paste into the hot pudding. Make meringue and spoon over the pudding. Bake at 350°F until meringue gets golden tips.

CORN MEAL MUSH WITH COCONUT MILK
(Tembleque de Harina de Maíz)

1 small can coconut milk	½ teaspoon salt
1 can water	7 tablespoons cornmeal
1 cup milk	1 stick cinnamon
1 tablespoon butter	

Mix all ingredients together and cook over low heat, stirring with wooden spoon until mixture separates from the sides of the pot. You may add raisins during the last minutes of cooking. Pour on a platter and sprinkle top with ground cinnamon.

EGG CUSTARD
(Tocinillo)

CUSTARD

Caramelize the mold with 1 cup sugar and ¼ cup water. After the caramel cools, butter the mold.

2 cups sugar	1 teaspoon vanilla
1 cup water	1 can condensed milk
12 egg yolks	¼ teaspoon salt
6 egg whites	

Boil water and sugar for 15 minutes to make a syrup. Cool. Beat the 12 egg yolks with the 6 egg whites. Add salt, vanilla and condensed milk. Slowly add the syrup to the egg mixture, mixing well. Pour in the caramelized mold and set the mold in a large pan with about 1 inch of water. Bake for 40 minutes at 350°F. Refrigerate before unmolding.

COCONUT CUSTARD
(Flan de Coco)

1 cup fresh coconut milk	¾ cups sugar
1 cup milk	¼ teaspoon salt
2 egg yolks	6 tablespoons cornstarch

Beat egg yolks, sugar, salt and cornstarch together until creamy. Add milk and coconut milk. Cook over low heat, stirring constantly until cream thickens. Pour in a caramelized mold and refrigerate before unmolding.

COCONUT CUSTARD "LUCHI"
(Flan de Dulce de Coco "Luchi")

6 eggs	1 teaspoon vanilla
1 can coconut in syrup	2 tablespoons rum
1 cup milk	dash salt
1 can evaporated milk	

Beat eggs, add all the other ingredients mixing well. Pour in a caramelized mold and place the mold in a larger pan with about 1 inch of water. Bake at 350°F for 1 hour. Refrigerate before unmolding.

PEACH CUSTARD "MIMI"
(Flan de Melocotón "Mimi)

2 boxes strawberry gelatin	1 (1 lb. 4 oz.) can peaches in syrup
2 cups hot water	1 can condensed milk
1 (8 oz) can peach nectar	

Dissolve gelatin in hot water. Puree peaches with the syrup in a blender or put through a sieve and mix well with the gelatin, the peach nectar and condensed milk. Pour in a caramelized mold and refrigerate for 12 hours before unmolding. You can substitute with other flavors - lime, lemon, orange....

CHEESE CUSTARD "RINA"
(Flan de Queso "Rina")

3 eggs
1 can condensed milk
1 stick butter - melted
1 (8 oz) cream cheese

CARAMEL FOR MOLD
1 ½ cups sugar
½ cup water

To caramelize the mold, heat water and sugar until syrup is golden. Set aside. Beat eggs, add all the other ingredients and mix well. Pour through a sieve into the caramelized mold, cover with aluminum foil and set the mold in a large pan with water 1 inch deep. Bake at 350°F for 45 minutes. Refrigerate and unmold.

IMPERIAL CREAM "GUAMÁ"
(Crema Imperial "Guamá")

4 egg yolks
¾ cup sugar
½ teaspoon salt
6 tablespoons cornstarch

3 cups milk
peel of 1 green lemon
1 Sponge Cake
1 cup sweet wine – Sherry, Madeira, Port

MERINGUE
4 egg whites   4 tablespoons sugar

Beat egg yolks with sugar, salt and cornstarch. Meanwhile, simmer milk with lemon peel. Mix about 1 cup warm milk with the beaten egg yolks. Add to the other warm milk and cook, stirring until cream thickens. If the cream gets lumpy, beat vigorously to get rid of the lumps. Thinly slice the Sponge Cake. Arrange cake slices on a platter or shallow mold and drizzle with the wine. Pour the egg cream over the cake slices. Make meringue and spoon over the cream You may also drizzle caramelized sugar over the egg cream before the meringue. Bake in 350°F oven for 8 to 10 minutes or until meringue tops get golden.

PUMPKIN CUSTARD "LILLIAN"
(Flan de Calabaza "Lillian")

4 eggs	1 lb. pumpkin
1 cup milk	2 ½ tablespoons flour
1 cup sugar	Grated green lemon peel

Boil pumpkin in salted water. Beat eggs. Drain pumpkin and add to eggs. Add the other ingredients, beat in the blender or put through a sieve. Pour in a caramelized mold. Set the mold in a large pan with about 1 inch of water. Bake at 350°F until a knife or a cake tester emerge clean. Refrigerate and unmold. Keep refrigerated.

PUMPKIN CUSTARD "MAMAI"
(Flan de Calabaza "Mamai")

2 lbs. pumpkin	1 ½ cups sugar
1 small box cornstarch (10 tablespoons)	1 teaspoon vanilla
1 can evaporated milk	

Boil pumpkin in salted water and reserve. Mix the evaporated milk with fresh milk to complete 1 quart. Measure 1 cup of this milk, mix with the cornstarch mixture and reserve to be used later. Mix the remaining milk with the pumpkin, sugar and vanilla in a blender or put through a sieve and heat until it simmers, stirring constantly. Add the milk and cornstarch mixture and cook stirring constantly until the mixture thickens and separates from the sides of the pan. Pour in a caramelized mold. Refrigerate and unmold.
Note: The pumpkin used is the tropical or creole pumpkin, which is different from the Halloween pumpkin or the squash. It is available in Spanish markets.

MOTHER'S VOL-AU-VENT
(Buñuelos de Viento de Mamá)

2 cups water + 2 teaspoons sugar	2 cups flour
1 stick butter	2 teaspoons baking powder
½ teaspoon salt	8 whole eggs
anise seeds	2 egg yolks

Bring water to a boil with salt, sugar, butter and anise seeds. Remove anise seeds. Add the flour and baking powder- sifted together, all at once, stirring vigorously until mixture forms a ball. Remove from heat, cool and add whole eggs, one at a time, beating well after each addition. Add the egg yolks and beat well. Drop from a teaspoon into hot oil, about 6 or 8 at a time. As fritters rise to the surface pierce with a fork, then cover pan until they puff and take golden color.

SYRUP

4 cups sugar	1 stick cinnamon
1 cup water	

Boil together until desired thickness. Serve Vol-Au-Vent and spoon syrup over each serving.

BAKED PUFFS
(Buñuelos de Viento Horneados)

2 cups water	**SYRUP**
1/2 lb. margarine	
2 cups flour - unsifted	3 cups sugar
1/2 teaspoon salt	3 cups water
8 whole eggs	green lemon peel

Bring water to a boil with salt and margarine. Add flour, al at once, and beat with wooden spoon until batter separates from the sides of the pan. Remove from heat. Beat and add eggs, one at a time, beating well after each addition. Drop from a teaspoon on greased baking sheets and bake at 375' F for 40 minutes. To make syrup boil sugar, water & lemon peel until thick. Cool slightly and drizzle over puffs.

PUMPKIN PUDDING "SAN MARTÍN"
(Budín de Calabaza "San Martín")

1 1/2 cups fresh coconut milk
2 cups mashed boiled pumpkin
2 cups sugar
5 eggs
1/2 cup milk

¾ cup cornstarch (1 small box)
1 teaspoon cinnamon
1 tablespoon baking powder
6 tablespoons butter
1 teaspoon vanilla

Mix all ingredients together. Pour in buttered mold and bake at 350°F for 1 hour. Note: The pumpkin used is the tropical or creole pumpkin, which is different from the Halloween pumpkin or the squash. It is available in Spanish markets.

MILK FUDGE "MARIANNE"
(Dulce de Leche "Maríanne")

1 quart milk
1 3/4 cups sugar

Green lemon peel from whole lemon

Mix all ingredients and heat until almost to a boil, then simmer, stirring constantly for about 1 1/2 hours, scraping the bottom of the pot to prevent from sticking and scorching. Test by dropping a small amount of the mixture in ice water, f the mixture forms a ball and holds its shape and does not flatten, it is done (242' to 248' F on a candy thermometer). Remove from heat and beat until creamy. Pour on a marble slab or a large ungreased Pyrex mold. Let cool and cut in cubes. Store in tin cans.

FUDGE "DOÑA ASUNCIÓN"
(Fudge "Doña Asunción")

3 oz. unsweetened chocolate
2 cans evaporated milk
2 cans water

1 teaspoon vanilla
3 ½ cups sugar
4 tablespoons butter

Mix all ingredients together in a large heavy pot, large enough that the candy does not overflow when it boils. Stir constantly to prevent from sticking. As candy thickens, beat more vigorously. Test by dropping a small amount in ice water until it reaches the ball stage. Remove from heat and beat until creamy. Pour on a buttered platter until firm, then cut in squares. Store in tin cans.

TASTES SO GOOD "MAMACHITA"
(Bien Me Sabe "Mamachita")

1 ½ cups fresh or canned coconut milk
9 egg yolks
3 cups sugar + ¾ cups water
1 stick cinnamon

Boil water, sugar and cinnamon together pork meat roll Let cool. Beat egg yolks until creamy, add coconut milk, then sugar syrup and simmer stirring constantly until the mixture thickens to coat a spoon. Serve as topping with Sponge Cake. Canned coconut milk is available in Spanish markets. To make fresh coconut milk, wrap the coconut in a kitchen towel and crack open, catching the water as coconut breaks. Pry out the coconut meat and grind in a blender or food processor, adding the coconut water or tap water. Squeeze in a clean cloth.

PUDDING "BONO"
(Budín "Bono")

1 lb. French bread
1 quart milk
1 1/3 cups sugar
1 small box raisins
6 whole eggs
1 teaspoon cinnamon
1/2 cup Sherry wine
1 teaspoon vanilla
1/2 stick butter - melted

Soak bread in milk. Mix together all ingredients, reserving the raisins to be added later. Pour the mixture in a well buttered mold. Push raisins into the batter. Bake at 325°F for 1 1/2 hours and top is golden.

BREADFRUIT PUDDING
(Budín de Panapén)

2 cups mashed breadfruit
4 cups fresh coconut milk
1 1/2 cups sugar
1/3 cup flour
4 beaten eggs
4 tablespoons melted butter
1 teaspoon vanilla
CARAMEL
1 ½ cups sugar
1/3 cup water

Caramelize the mold. Mix all ingredients and pour through a sieve into a mold. Set the mold in a larger mold with 1 inch of water. Bake at 350' for 1 hour or until a cake tester or a knife emerge clean. Let stand until cool. Refrigerate and unmold.

BREAD PUDDING WITH FRUITS
(Budín de Pan con Frutas)

2 lbs. white (sandwich) bread	3 oz. butter – softened
1 quart milk	6 beaten eggs
1/2 teaspoon salt	1 can fruit cocktail in syrup – drained
1 teaspoon grated green lemon peel	1 can sliced pineapple in syrup - drained
1 teaspoon vanilla	1 can maraschino cherries
2 cups sugar	

Beat eggs, add milk, bread, salt, lemon peel, vanilla, sugar and butter. Whirl in a blender or put through a sieve. Add drained fruit cocktail. Caramelize a mold and line with drained pineapple slices and maraschino cherries. Pour pudding mixture over pineapple slices. Place the mold in a larger mold with 1 inch deep water. Bake at 400'F for 1 hour Refrigerate and unmold.

BRANDY BALLS
(Bolitas de Brandy)

2 tablespoons unsweetened cocoa	2 tablespoons white Karo syrup
1 cup Confectioners' sugar - sifted	2 ½ cups Graham cracker crumbs
1/2 cup Brandy	

Knead all ingredients together and shape into balls. Roll in Confectioners' sugar. Store in well covered tin cans for at least 12 hours before serving.

RUM BALLS
(Bolitas de Ron)

2 cups Graham cracker crumbs – sifted	1 1/ cups white Karo syrup
1 cup Confectioners sugar – sifted	¼ cup rum

Combine crumbs and Confectioners' sugar. Add Karo syrup and rum, and knead well. Shape into balls. Roll in Confectioners' sugar. You may flavor the Confectioners' sugar with cocoa or with instant coffee. Also you may substitute rum with Cointreau or whiskey. Store in well covered tin cans for at least 12 hours before using.

TÍO PEPE'S BREAD PUDDING
(Budín de Pan "Tío Pepe")

1 lb. French bread	1 teaspoon vanilla
1 (15 oz) can evaporated milk	1 teaspoon ground cinnamon
2 cups sugar	1 teaspoon ground cloves
2 beaten eggs	¼ cup rum
3 tablespoons butter - melted	¼ cup red wine
2 tablespoons vegetable oil	½ cup raisins

Soak bread in evaporated milk, adding enough water as needed to soften bread. Reserve raisins to be used later. Mix all the other ingredients together with the bread, stirring with a wooden spoon or a fork until well mixed. Pour in a buttered mold. Place the raisins over the batter, spacing them apart and pushing them into the batter. Bake at 375' for 1 hour and the top is brown.

GUAVA SHELLS CANDY "CALLE LUNA"
(Casquitos da Guayaba "Calle Luna")

5 lbs. ripe guavas (hard to the touch)	4 cups sugar
7 cups water	

Wash and peel guavas. A vegetable peeler works very well. Reserve the guava peels to make jelly. Cut guavas in half and scoop out the seeds. Reserve seeds. Boil the guava shells in 7 cups water for 25 minutes. Do not stir. Add the sugar and let come to a boil. Do not stir. Turn heat down and simmer, uncovered, for 1 1/2 hours. Sometimes, the candy is done before the time is up. Watch carefully after 1 hour and test by dipping a teaspoon in the syrup, wait until cool to the touch, pick some syrup with the tip of your index finger and if it feels sticky, that is the right stage. If you are using white guavas, although they are not the best for candy making, add a few drops of red food color.

PUDDING "TWIN BELLS"
(Cazuela "Dos Campanas")

2 cups white sweet potatoes boiled
2 cups pumpkin - boiled
1/2 ripe plantain- boiled
4 beaten eggs
1/4 cup flour
1/4 cup rice meal

¼ cup melted butter
3 – 4 tablespoons Brandy
1 2/2 cups sugar
1 cup fresh coconut milk
2 tablespoons ground cinnamon
¾ (2 tsp.) tablespoons ground cloves

Buy 2 lbs. sweet potatoes and 2 lbs. pumpkin to boil in water and salt. Drain well before mashing. Mix all ingredients together in a blender or put through a sieve. Pour in a well buttered mold and bake at 350°F for 2 hours.

COCONUT DELIGHT
(Merengada de Coco)

COCONUT DELIGHT PUDDING
2 grated coconuts
3 cups sugar
3 tablespoons water
4 egg yolks
1 cup evaporated milk

MERINGUE
4 egg whites
1 ½ cups sugar
1/2 cup water
1 teaspoon white Karo syrup
1 teaspoon vanilla
3 tablespoons sugar

Bring to a boil the grated coconut with the sugar and the 3 tablespoons water. Add the evaporated milk and simmer until mixture thickens and separates from the sides of the pan. Remove from heat and let cool down. Add egg yolks, one at a time, beating well after each addition. Pour in a platter or mold. Cover with meringue. Make a syrup with 1/2 cup water and 1 1/2 cups sugar and Karo syrup. Beat egg whites, stiff but not dry. Add the 3 tablespoons sugar and the vanilla, then add the hot syrup in a thin stream, very slowly and beating continuously. Continue beating until meringue stands in peaks. Spoon meringue over the Coconut Delight, from the edges toward the center, to prevent shrinkage. Bake until the meringue tips are golden.

GRANDMA'S LOVE DUST
(Polvo de Amor "Abuelita")

Mix the grated coconut (after you have squeezed out the milk) with about 2 cups sugar. You may use 1 cup white sugar and 1 cup brown sugar. Cook on high heat stirring continuously until sugar is melted. Turn heat to low and cook about 15 minutes longer, stirring frequently until golden. Cool and store in tightly covered glass jars. You can use Love Dust sprinkled over cakes, ice cream, fruits, or as is.

THE BIG MERINGUE "WADED"
(Merengón "Waded")

10 egg whites	**CARAMEL**
1 3/4 cups sugar	1 cup sugar
1/4 teaspoon cream of tartar	¼ cup water

Preheat oven to 450' F.

In a tube cake mold heat sugar and water until golden, turning mold around to coat sides and using a spoon to coat the tube also. When the caramel cools brush butter over caramel. Beat the egg whites together with cream of tartar until stiff but not dry. Add sugar one tablespoon at a time, beating continuously until all the sugar is absorbed. Spoon meringue into cake mold and draw a knife or a spatula through the meringue to get rid of large air pockets. Smooth top and immediately put in hot 450' oven and turn the oven OFF. Leave the meringue undisturbed for 4 hours. Remove from oven and as soon as cool enough to handle, gently separate from the sides and the center of the mold. Invert on a platter. You can serve as is or with a topping of Egg Cream, Chocolate Cream, Tastes So Good (Bien Me Sabe "Mamachita") or fresh strawberries or other fruits.

EGG CREAM "DOÑA YUYA"
(Natilla "doña Yuya")

2 cups sugar
1 quart milk
1 can evaporated milk
8 egg yolks

6 heaping teaspoons cornstarch
1 stick cinnamon
1 lemon peel (from whole lemon)

Mix the two milks and heat together with the cinnamon stick, lemon peel and sugar. Beat egg yolks with cornstarch and vanilla until creamy. Slowly stir about 1 cup hot milk into the egg yolks. Add this mixture to the hot milk. Simmer, stirring continuously to keep from scorching and from getting lumps. Cook until the cream thickens. Pour in bowls or glass cups and refrigerate. Sprinkle with cinnamon.

PUDDING "TÍA BEBÉ"
(Pantizo "Tía Bebé")

1 loaf white bread - remove crust
1 1/2 quarts milk
4 egg yolks
1 cup sugar
4 green lemons - grated
1/2 teaspoon salt
1 guava paste

CARAMEL
Boil 1 cup sugar and 1/4 cup water, lower heat and cook until slightly thick. Caramelize the mold.

Caramelize mold. Soak the bread in the milk. Beat together ©99 yolks and sugar. Add soaked bread with the milk, grated lemon peel of 4 lemons and salt, mixing well. Pour in the caramelized mold. Set the mold in a large pan with 1 inch of water. Bake in hot 350' oven for 20 minutes. Remove from oven and push thin guava slices deep into the half cooked batter. Return to oven for 40 minutes or until tester emerges clean. Refrigerate and unmold.

MARZIPAN APPLES "ZOÉ"
(Manzanas de Almendras "Zoé")

1 lb. almonds - skinned	1 ¼ lb. sugar
12 egg yolks	¾ cup water

Boil sugar and water to make a very heavy syrup. In the blender or food processor, grind the almonds, add egg yolks, one at a time, until very well blended, very creamy and compact. Add the syrup slowly, and cook in a heavy pot, on very low heat until dough can be shaped into a ball when a small amount is rolled between two fingers. Add red food coloring and mix well. Pour dough on a marble slab or on a platter. Flatten dough with a rolling pin, then shape into small balls to simulate apples. Stick a whole clove at one end to simulate a stem.

DON JULIÁN'S LEMON PIE
(Pie de Limón "don Julián")

2 frozen pie shells.
Bake following package instructions and cool before filling.

FILLING FOR 2 PIES

6 egg yolks	3 cups sugar
1 1/8 cups cornstarch	2 teaspoons salt
3 1/4 cups water	3 oz. butter

3/8 cup lime juice (use only green lemons)

Mix together all ingredients, except the butter, and put through a sieve. Cook on very low heat, add butter and continue cooking until very creamy and thickened. Pour half of the mixture into each pie crust.

MERINGUE

6 egg whites	1 1/8 cups sugar

Beat egg whites until soft peaks, stiff but not dry. Beat in sugar, one tablespoon at a time, until all the sugar is used. Spoon meringue on pie filling, from the edges towards the center, to prevent meringue from pulling away during baking. Bake at 325' F for 10 to 15 minutes. Cool before serving.

MARSHMALLOW SYRUP "EVAN"
(Sirop de Marshmallow "Evan")

1 cup white Karo syrup
1 cup water
1 cup sugar

3 egg whites
½ teaspoon vanilla

Boil water, sugar and Karo syrup until syrup reaches the thread stage. When the spoon is lifted from the hot syrup and the last drops form a very thin thread, that is the thread stage. If you own a thermometer, 230°F is the right temperature. Beat the egg whites until stiff. Add syrup to the beaten egg whites, slowly and beating all the time. Add vanilla and beat until thickened.

MARSHMALLOW SYRUP "Tía Mercedes"
(Sirop de Marshmallow "Tía Mercedes")

¼ cup water
3/4 cup sugar
1/3 cup white Karo syrup

½ teaspoon vanilla
2 egg whites

Boil sugar, water and Karo syrup together until syrup reaches the thread stage - about 230°F on a candy thermometer- or when a thread forms as you lift a spoon from the syrup. Beat the egg whites until stiff but not dry. Add hot syrup in a very thin stream, slowly and beating continuously. Add vanilla and continue beating until thickened.

COCONUT CREAM "LIVIA I"
(Tembleque "Livia I")

2 cups milk
2 cups coconut milk
1 small box cornstarch (¾ cup)
1 cup sugar

½ teaspoon salt
1 cinnamon stick
1 sprig tender orange or lime leaves

Mix milk, coconut milk, salt and sugar. In a separate bowl measure about 1 cup of this mixture, add the cornstarch, mix and reserve for later use. Boil the first mixture with the orange or lime leaves and cinnamon stick. Add slowly the cornstarch mixture, stirring, and simmer stirring all the time until mixture separates from the sides of the pan. Pour In a platter or mold and sprinkle with ground cinnamon. Cool. To serve cut in squares.

GUAVA JELLY "PORTA COELI"
(Jalea de Guayaba "Porta Coeli")

Use the guava peelings and the seeds that you reserved when making Guava Shells Candy.

3 lbs. guava peels and seeds
6 cups water

3 cups sugar

Simmer guava peels and seeds with the 6 cups water, for 25 minutes, stirring often to prevent scorching. Strain and pour through a cloth or a jelly bag. Measure 3 cups liquid, add 3 cups sugar, stir and boil for 15 minutes. If you use a candy thermometer the temperature should read 224' F. Place a teaspoon in each jar to absorb the heat so that the jars will not break. Pour the hot syrup into the jars. Place lids on jars and cool before refrigerating. If you do not use a candy thermometer, the jelly stage takes about 15 minutes of rapid boiling and when a spoon is lifted the syrup will fall in 2 thick drops.

SAN GERMAN'S FLOATING ISLAND
(Isla Flotante "Sangermeña")

4 egg yolks 3/4 cup sugar	3 cups milk
1/2 teaspoon salt	Peel of 1 or 2 green lemons

Simmer milk with lemon peel for about 15 to 20 minutes. Beat egg yolks with sugar and salt. Add some of the hot milk to the egg yolks, stirring, then add this mixture to the simmering milk and cook until cream thickens and coats the spoon. If you want a thicker cream add about 1 teaspoon cornstarch. Pour in glass cups and refrigerate.

THE ISLANDS

4 egg whites	1 guava paste

Heat guava paste with about 1 tablespoon water and mash with a fork. Beat the egg whites until stiff. Slowly add hot guava paste, always beating, adding enough guava paste to suit your taste. Drop a large spoonful of this meringue in each cup, on top of the cream to simulate the island. Serve very cold.

CREAM OF RICE "YAVITA"
(Majarete "Yavita")

5 cups fresh coconut milk	**TO MAKE COCONUT MILK**
1 cup rice meal	Crack open a coconut, wrapped in a kitchen towel.
1 teaspoon salt	Catch the water I a bowl as coconut breaks. Pry
1 tablespoon lard	out the coconut meat and grind in the blender or
1 1/4 cups sugar	food processor, adding the coconut water and hot
3 sticks cinnamon	water as needed. Squeeze in clean cloth or
green lemon peel - from 1	cheesecloth. If preferred may purchase canned
whole lemon	coconut milk.

Mix all ingredients and simmer stirring continuously. Do not stop stirring or the mixture will stick to the pan. Simmer, stirring, until mixture bursts in bubbles and separates from the sides of the pan. Pour in a platter and sprinkle with ground cinnamon.

MAYE'S MERINGUES
(Merengues "Maye")

1 cup egg whites
3 cups sugar

1 teaspoon vanilla   or
½ teaspoon grated lemon peel

Butter or oil the baking sheets and line with wax paper. Do not butter wax paper. Beat egg whites until stiff. Add sugar, a tablespoon at a time, add vanilla or lemon peel, beating until all the sugar is used. Drop meringues from a teaspoon on the baking sheets. Bake at 250°F for about 12 minutes and crispy on the outside. Do not brown. Remove baking sheets from oven, wait a few seconds, pick the wax paper at one end and invert on a kitchen towel, removing meringues. You may color meringues by adding food coloring as you beat egg whites with the sugar.

MANGO PASTE "COTUÍ"
(Pasta de Mangó "Cotuí")

Wash ripe, hard to the touch mangoes. Cut off stem ends. Do not peel. Boil until soft and drain overnight to get rid of all the liquid. The next day, peel the boiled mangoes and scrape the meat or pulp into a bowl. Strain pulp and measure. For each cup mango pulp add 1 cup sugar. Simmer this mixture, stirring continuously until it separates from the sides of the pan. Pour in molds and refrigerate, covered with paper towels, until set and the tops feel dry to the touch. Keeps well in the refrigerator. Can also be frozen for later use, wrapped in plastic wrap and aluminum foil.

CHANTILLY "DIDÍ"
(Chantilly "Didí")

2 cups sugar
3/4 cup evaporated milk
1 cup milk

2 tablespoons Karo syrup
1/8 teaspoon salt
1 teaspoon vanilla

Cook ingredients together until syrup reaches 250°F on a candy thermometer or to the soft ball stage. Remove from heat, add 1 teaspoon vanilla and beat vigorously until very creamy. Pour on a buttered platter. When cold cut in squares.

WHITE FUDGE "DIVINITY"
(Fudge Blanco "Divinity")

2 egg whites	½ cup white Karo syrup
½ cup water	2 cups sugar

You may also use brown sugar but you must then add 1 tablespoon vinegar. You will not call it "Divinity" and you cannot call it White Fudge.

Boil Karo syrup, water and sugar, covered, for 3 minutes. Watch that the sugar crystals that form on the sides of the pan, melt into the syrup. Remove the lid and let boil until a hard ball forms when a small amount of syrup is dropped in a saucer with ice water. Beat egg whites until stiff but not dry, add hot syrup in a very thin stream, beating all the time, until mixture hardens. Drop from a teaspoon on a buttered platter or marble slab.

SWEET POTATO CANDY
(Dulce de Batata "Yuyú")

2 lbs. yellow sweet potatoes	1 cup coconut milk
¾ lb. sugar	¼ teaspoon almond extract

Boil unpeeled sweet potatoes. Peel and mash. Add coconut milk and sugar. Mix well and cook over low heat, stirring frequently with a wooden spoon, until mixtures separates from the sides of the pan and when a small amount rolled between your fingers forms a ball. Remove from heat and pour on a platter and cool for 10 to 12 hours. Add almond extract, knead well and shape into rolls 2 1/2 to 3 inches long, finger shape or in small balls. Roll in ground cinnamon. You can stick a whole clove at one end of each ball to simulate a stem.

Cookies… Cakes… Icings…

Oh Lord, may Your love for
all mankind, be visible
and tangible in me....

MAMA CELIA'S UPSIDE DOWN CAKE
(Bizcocho al Revés "Mamá Celia")

1 1/2 sticks butter 1 1/4 cups sugar	2 ½ cups sifted flour
8 egg yolks	1 cup brown sugar
4 teaspoons baking powder	Canned apricots – drained
1 teaspoon vanilla 3/4 cup milk	Canned pineapple slices - drained
	Maraschino cherries – drained

Grease a shallow cake mold and sprinkle with the brown sugar. Arrange drained fruits over the brown sugar. Beat butter and sugar until creamy. In a separate bowl beat the egg yolks until creamy, add to the butter mixture and beat well. Sift dry ingredients together and add to the creamed mixture, alternating with the milk, starting and ending with flour. Add vanilla. Pour in the cake mold, over the fruits. Bake at 350°F for 45 to 60 minutes. Test for doneness. Let stand for 3 minutes and unmold.

COFFEE AND NUTS CAKE
(Bizcocho de Café y Nueces)

1 1/2 cups sugar 1/2 lb. butter	½ teaspoon vanilla
4 egg yolks	½ cup flour
9 tablespoons evaporated milk	3 teaspoons baking soda
3 tablespoons strong black coffee	¾ cups chopped nuts
	¾ cup chopped dates

Beat egg yolks, butter and sugar until creamy. Add milk, coffee and vanilla, beating until well mixed. Fold in sifted dry ingredients, nuts and dates. Pour in a greased cake pan. Bake at 325°F for 1 hour. Cool and glaze.

GLAZE *(for Coffee and Nuts Cake)*

5 egg whites	1 teaspoon lime juice
7 cups Confectioners' sugar	4 drops food coloring

Beat ingredients together, slowly, for 15 minutes. To make a thicker icing to decorate borders, add more Confectioners' sugar until icing holds its shape.

SPICE CAKE WITH SWEET WINE
(Bizcocho de Especias con Vino Dulce)

1 cup flour	½ lb. butter
3 teaspoons baking powder	1 teaspoon vanilla
3 teaspoons ground cinnamon	¾ cup milk
1 teaspoon ground cloves	6 eggs – separated
1 teaspoon ground nutmeg	½ cup sweet wine
2 cups brown sugar	

Sift dry ingredients together three times. Beat margarine with sugar, egg yolks and vanilla. Mix wine and milk. Add alternating with the dry ingredients. Beat egg whites until stiff and fold in. Pour in a buttered 10 inch tube mild and bake at 350 ' F for 40 minutes.

SPONGE CAKE
(Bizcocho Esponjoso)

6 eggs – separated	½ teaspoon salt
1 cup sugar	2 tablespoons lemon juice
1 cup flour	½ teaspoon grated lemon peel
½ teaspoon baking powder	

Beat egg yolks until creamy, add sugar a spoonful at a time, until well blended. Mix in lemon juice and grated lemon peel. Beat egg whites until stiff. Fold in half of the beaten egg whites into the egg yolks, then fold in dry ingredients, sifted together. Fold in the reserved egg whites. Pour in an ungreased 10 Inch tube cake pan.
Bake at 350' F for 45 minutes.

LACE COOKIES
(Encajitos)

¼ lb. margarine
1 ½ cups oatmeal - not instant
1 teaspoon flour
1 teaspoon baking powder

½ teaspoon salt
¾ cups sugar
2 teaspoons vanilla
1 beaten egg

Melt butter and mix together with the first 5 ingredients, then add egg and vanilla and mix well. Drop dough from a teaspoon on a baking sheet lines with aluminum foil. Bake at 325°F for 12 to 15 minutes or until they start to brown.

MOIST CAKE "CARMEN LUISA"
(Bizcocho Mojado "Carmen Luisa")

2 cups sugar
1 cup water
lemon peel or lemon extract
6 eggs - separated

6 tablespoons sugar
6 tablespoons flour
½ teaspoon baking powder
1 teaspoon vanilla

Boil 2 cups sugar with 1 cup water and lemon peel or lemon extract to make a thin syrup. Beat until creamy 6 egg yolks with the 6 tablespoons sugar. Beat egg whites until stiff and fold into the egg yolks. Sift together flour and baking powder and fold into the egg mixture. Add vanilla. Pour the boiling syrup in a shallow glass cake mold and immediately pour the cake batter over the hot syrup. Bake in hot oven at 350°F for 20 to 30 minutes. Remove from oven, separate cake from sides of cake pan but do not unmold.

DON PEDRO'S MARZIPAN CAKE
(Bizcocho Mazapán "don Pedro")

6 egg whites
12 egg yolks
2 cups sugar

1 lb. skinned ground almonds
1/4 lb. flour
1/2 cup sweet wine

Beat egg whites until stiff, add egg yolks, one at a time, beating well after each addition. Add sugar and beat well. Add chopped almonds and wine. Fold in flour. Pour batter in a buttered cake pan. Bake at 350' for 40 to 45 minutes or until cake tester emerges clean.

APPLE CAKE "DIN"
(Bizcocho de Manzana "Din")

2 cups cake flour	**GLAZE**
1 cup raisins	3 tablespoons butter
1 cup sugar	5 tablespoons brown sugar
1 cup chopped nuts	2 tablespoons milk cream or evaporated milk
1 teaspoon salt	Mix together and spread over hot cake. Return
1 teaspoon ground cinnamon	to oven until glaze bubbles
1 teaspoon baking soda	
1/2 teaspoon ground cloves	
1/2 cup butter	
1 beaten egg	
1 cup apple sauce- drained	

Sift together flour, baking soda and spices. Beat together butter and sugar. Add beaten egg and mix well, Add dry ingredients alternating with apple sauce and beat until well mixed. Fold in nuts and raisins. Pour in buttered cake mold and bake at 350°F for 1 hour. Glaze while still hot.

MY VERY OWN MAZAPANES
(Mazapanes "Los Míos")

12 egg yolks	1 tablespoon Crisco
2 1/4 cups sugar	½ teaspoon ground cinnamon
1 1/2 cups sifted flour	¾ teaspoon almond extract
3 tablespoons butter	1 tablespoon ice water

Preheat oven to 375° F. Beat all ingredients together only until mixed. Do not over—beat. Have ready well buttered muffin tins, using softened butter. Pour about 1 teaspoon of the batter in each muffin tin. Bake for 8 to 10 minutes. Do not brown. Unmold immediately because they are hard to unmold when cold.

meal CAKE "CARMENCITA"
(Bizcocho Moka "Carmencita")

4 eggs - separated	1 stick butter - melted
1 cup flour	2 tablespoons instant coffee
3/4 cup sugar	1 tablespoon water

Beat egg whites until foamy. Add sugar, a tablespoon at a time, then egg yolks, one at a time, beating well after each addition. Mix instant coffee with 1 tablespoon water and add to the batter. Beat in flour and melted butter, mixing until well blended. Pour in buttered cake pan and bake at 350° F for 30 minutes.

SYRUP *(for Mocha Cake Carmencita)*

3/4 cup water	Boil water and sugar 1 minute. Cool,
3/4 cup sugar	add Cognac and reserve until needed
1/4 cup Cognac	

MOCHA ICING *(for Mocha Cake Carmencita)*

2 1/2 sticks butter	2 tablespoons instant coffee
2 cups Confectioners' sugar	1 tablespoon water
3 egg yolks	

Beat butter and sugar until creamy. Add egg yolks one at a time, beating well after each addition. Mix 2 tablespoons instant coffee with 1 tablespoon water and add to the batter, beating for 3 minutes. Slice cake, place a layer of cake slices in a glass dish, drizzle with syrup, spread with Mocha Icing, again cake, syrup and end with cake slices. Spread icing over cake.

ICE BOX CAKE "CARITA"
(Bizcocho de Nevera "Carita")

1 sponge cake	1 teaspoon vanilla
4 eggs - separated	Sherry wine
1 cup sugar	Red & green maraschino cherries
1/2 lb. butter	1 can crushed pineapple
60 to 70 ladyfingers	

Beat sugar and butter until creamy. Add egg yolks one at a time, beating well. Crumb cake pulling apart with fingers. Add cake crumbs to egg mixture. Beat egg whites until foamy and fold into the batter. Butter a cake mold and line with wax paper, moisten ladyfingers with wine one at a time and line bottom and sides of the cake mold with the ladyfingers, placing them flat on the bottom of the mold, and standing with the curved sides against the mold. Do not moisten ladyfingers too much because they will disintegrate. Spoon filling carefully over ladyfingers, alternate with crushed pineapple, then again with moistened ladyfingers, again filling and top with ladyfingers. Moisten the top layer of ladyfingers with the wine after they have been placed on top of the filling. Wrap mold in plastic wrap or wax paper and freeze for 20 to 24 hours. When ready to serve, remove from freezer and invert on a cold plate until it unmolds itself.

HOT MILK CAKE Mrs. Pelz
(Bizcocho de Leche Caliente Mrs. Pelz

4 eggs	1 cup hot milk
2 cups sugar	1 teaspoon
2 cups flour	2 teaspoons baking powder
1/4 lb. butter	

Bring milk and butter to a boil. Beat eggs, add sugar, a spoonful at a time, beating well after each addition. Add flour, alternately with the hot milk, ending with flour. Add vanilla. Mix in baking powder. Do not over beat. Bake in a well buttered cake pan at 350°F for 1 hour.

WITCHES POUND CAKE
(Ponqué Brujo)

8 egg whites - beaten stiff with
1 ½ cups sugar – added slowly
In a separate bowl – beat 8 egg yolks
Add 1 tablespoon brandy, whiskey or rum
2 cups flour – sifted together with
1 teaspoon baking powder
Add – ½ lb. melted butter

Fold the above mixture into beaten egg whites. Pour in a buttered cake pan and bake at 350°F for 45 minutes.

SYRUP *(for Witches Pound Cake)*

1 cup pineapple juice	Boil to make a thin syrup and while
1/2 cup sugar	syrup is still hot, spoon or drizzle over
3 tablespoons brandy, whiskey or rum	the cake.

BROWN COOKIES
(Galletitas Morenas)

2 cups brown sugar - packed	1 teaspoon cream of tartar
2 eggs	½ cup (2 sticks) butter
2 1/2 to 3 cups flour	1 teaspoon vanilla
1 teaspoon baking soda	½ cup chopped nuts

Mix well all ingredients and drop from a teaspoon on buttered cookie sheets. Flatten. Bake at 350° F for 8 to 10 minutes.

SPONGE CAKE "LILA"
(Bizcocho Esponjoso "Lila")

8 eggs - separated
1 1/4 cups sugar
1 teaspoon vanilla

2 cups cake flour
2 tablespoons baking powder
2 sticks butter - melted

Beat egg whites until stiff. Add sugar, a spoonful at a time, and beat well. Add egg yolks, one at a time, beating well after each addition. Add vanilla and beat for 3 minutes. Sift flour together with baking powder and fold into the batter. Add melted butter all at once and beat only until mixed. Pour in a well buttered and floured cake pan. Bake at 325' F for 45 minutes.

CHRISTMAS COOKIES
(Galletitas de Navidad)

1/2 cup margarine
1/2 cup brown sugar - packed
1/2 cup granulated sugar
4 eggs
3 tablespoons milk
1/4 teaspoon salt
3 cups flour
2/3 cup rum, whiskey or brandy

1 teaspoon ground cloves
1 teaspoon ground cinnamon
1 teaspoon ground nutmeg
3 teaspoons baking soda
1 cup pecans or walnuts – chopped
1 cup raisins – chopped
1 cup dates - chopped

Mix well dry ingredients with butter, eggs and liquids. Mix in dry fruits and nuts. Drop from a teaspoon on a buttered cookie sheet. Bake at 325°F for 20 minutes or until done.

REFRIGERATOR COOKIES
(Galletitas de Nevera)

2 sticks margarine
1 ½ cups sugar
2 eggs
1 teaspoon vanilla

½ teaspoon salt
3 cups flour
½ teaspoon baking soda

Beat until creamy margarine, sugar, eggs, vanilla and salt. Add flour and baking soda. Knead and form into a ball. Refrigerate for 1 hour or longer. Roll with a rolling pin to ¼ inch thickness. Cut with a cookie cutter. Bake on an ungreased baking sheet at 350°F for 6 to 8 minutes.

MAZAPANES "AURORA"
(Mazapanes "Aurora")

10 egg yolks
¾ cup flour
1 ¼ cups sugar

4 to 6 teaspoons milk
2 oz. melted butter

Beat egg yolks with sugar until sugar is dissolved. Add melted butter, then flour alternating with milk. Pour from a teaspoon on well buttered and floured muffin tins. Bake at 450°F for 10 minutes. Unmold immediately.

COOKIES "ANA MARÍA"
(Mantecaditos "Ana María")

5 cups flour
2 teaspoons vanilla
1 lb. margarine

1 cup sugar
1 cup chopped nuts

Mix all ingredients and knead until dough holds together. Shape into walnut size balls and place on ungreased baking sheets. Bake at 325°F for 15 minutes.

DAINTY DATE COOKIES
(Delicias de Dátiles)

2 cups Corn Flakes or Bran Flakes
3/4 cup seedless dates - refrigerated
1/2 cup pecans
2 tablespoons honey
1 tablespoon butter
1 teaspoon lime juice
Confectioners sugar

In a meat grinder or food processor, grind the refrigerated dates, together with the cereal and pecans. Add margarine a lime juice. Knead until dough holds together. Shape into walnut size balls. Roll in Confectioners sugar

COOKIES "LEYLA ROSSY"
(Mantecaditos "Leyla Rossy")

1 lb. Crisco
2 cups sugar
2 eggs
1 teaspoon salt
6 cups flour
2 teaspoons vanilla or
1 teaspoon almond extract

Beat together Crisco and sugar. Add eggs, one at a time, salt and vanilla. Add flour. If using an electric mixer, when dough gets too stiff, knead with hands until dough holds together. Shape into walnut size balls, place on ungreased baking sheets and make a thumbprint on each cookie. Place a piece of guava paste on each thumbprint. Bake in hot oven at 325°F for 12 minutes. Do not brown.

COOKIES FROM SEVILLE
(Galletitas Sevillanas)

2 sticks butter
1 egg yolk
1 tablespoon Confectioners' sugar
1 tablespoon Cognac
2 cups sifted flour
½ teaspoon cinnamon
1 cup Confectioners sugar to coat cookies

Beat butter until creamy. In a separate bowl beat the egg yolk with 1 tablespoon Confectioners' sugar and Cognac. Add to the butter. Sift flour and cinnamon and add to the butter mixture. Knead dough using very little flour and shape into ovals 2x1 inches. Bake on ungreased cookie sheets at 350°F for 40 minutes. Cool for 2 to 3 minutes and immediately roll in Confectioners' sugar.

COWBOY COOKIES
(Galletitas "Vaquero")

1 cup margarine 1 cup sugar
1 cup brown sugar
2 cups flour
1 teaspoon baking powder
1/2 teaspoon salt
1 teaspoon baking soda
1 ½ cups oatmeal
1 cup chopped nuts
2 beaten eggs
1 cup grated coconut
1 teaspoon vanilla
1 ½ cups Rice Krispies cereal

Beat margarine and sugar together until creamy. Add eggs, vanilla, flour, baking powder, baking soda and salt. Beat well. Add oatmeal, coconut and nuts. Add Rice Krispies and mix. Shape into balls, place on ungreased cookie sheets and press to flatten. Bake at 350°F for 15 minutes.

SIMPLY COOKIES
(Simplemente Galletitas)

1 1/2 cups sugar
2/3 cup margarine
3 eggs
1/2 cup milk

3 ½ cups flour
3 teaspoons baking powder
1 teaspoon vanilla or lime juice

Beat until creamy margarine and sugar. Add eggs, one at a time, beating well after each addition. Sift together flour and baking powder and add to the egg mixture, alternating with milk. Add flavoring. Drop from a teaspoon on greased baking sheets. Butter bottom of a glass, then dip in sugar and press cookies to flatten. Bake at 325°F for 12 minutes.

NANÁ'S COOKIES
(Galletitas Naná)

4 sticks butter or margarine
1 cup sugar

4 cups + 1 tablespoon flour
¼ teaspoon salt

Beat all ingredients together and knead to a soft dough. Press the dough onto a shallow square or rectangular ungreased pan. Score top with a fork, making parallel or diagonal lines. Bake at 375°F oven for 1 1/2 hours. Remove from oven, cut immediately into bars about 2 x 1 inches. Turn oven OFF and return cookies to oven until it cools off.

CARAMEL ICING
(Azucarado de Caramelo)

1/4 cup margarine
1/2 cup brown sugar - packed

1/8 teaspoon salt
1/3 cup milk or evaporated milk

Cook all ingredients together in top of double boiler, stirring until smooth. Remove from hot water.

DATE FINGERS
(Dedos de Dátiles)

1/2 stick butter	1 teaspoon baking powder
1 cup sugar	1/2 teaspoon salt
3 beaten eggs	1 cup chopped dates
1 cup flour	1 cup chopped nuts (optional)
2 tablespoons Brandy	

Following given order mix ingredients together. Pour into a buttered and lined with wax paper square or rectangular pan. Bake at 350°F for 30 minutes.
Have ready a sheet of wax paper dusted with Confectioners' sugar. Remove cookies from oven, invert on the wax paper, cut in squares about 2x1 inches and roll immediately in the Confectioners' sugar.

CHOCOLATE COOKIES
(Galletitas de Chocolate)

1 package chocolate pudding	½ cup chopped nuts
2 cups firmly packed quick cooking oatmeal	¾ cup melted butter

Mix pudding, oatmeal and nuts. Add melted margarine and cut with two knives, then knead until dough holds together. Shape into walnut size balls and place on ungreased baking sheets. Score tops in a crisscross pattern with a fork.
Bake at 325° F for 10 minutes.

ORANGE GLAZE
(Azucarado de China)

3 cups Confectioners' sugar	4 tablespoons orange juice
3 tablespoons melted butter	1 tablespoon grated orange peel

Mix all ingredients together and use as cake filling and cake icing. You may add yellow food coloring.

EASY CHOCOLATE ICING
(Azucarado de Chocolate Fácil)

In top of double boiler melt:
3 ounces unsweetened chocolate
Remove from heat and add:

2 tablespoons margarine	1 teaspoon vanilla
2 3/4 cups Confectioners' sugar	6 tablespoons milk cream or
1/2 teaspoon salt	evaporated milk

Beat well together and return to double boiler for 10 minutes. If the icing thickens too much, add milk cream or evaporated milk until the desired consistency.

SPECIAL ICING
(Azucarado Especial)

1 cup sugar	1 teaspoon lemon juice
1/3 cup water	1 teaspoon vanilla
3 egg whites	Grated coconut (optional)

Boil water and sugar together for 10 minutes. Beat egg whites until stiff, add lemon juice and vanilla. When syrup reaches the thread stage, add very slowly to the beaten egg whites, beating constantly for 5 minutes. **When cool add:**
2 cups Confectioners' sugar   ½ teaspoon vanilla or 1 tablespoon rum
Beat until of spreading consistency.

BUTTER ICING
(Azucarado de Mantequilla)

1/4 cup butter	1 egg yolk
dash salt	½ teaspoon almond extract or vanilla
1 3/4 cups Confectioners' sugar - sifted	4 tablespoons milk

Beat all ingredients together until of spreading consistency.

BOILED ICING
(Azucarado do Hervido)

1/3 cup water
3/4 cup sugar
1/8 teaspoon cream of tartar
2 egg whites
½ teaspoon vanilla

Boil sugar, cream of tartar and water to the thread stage. Beat egg whites until stiff. Add syrup in a thin stream, beating constantly. Add vanilla and beat until of spreading consistency.

KARO ICING
(Azucarado de Karo)

¼ teaspoon salt
2 egg whites
¼ cup sugar
¾ cup white Karo syrup
1 ¼ teaspoons vanilla

Beat egg whites until stiff. Add sugar, a tablespoon at a time and continue beating until mixture is glossy. Slowly add Karo syrup and vanilla. Continue beating until icing reaches the desired consistency.

For variations add one of the following:
- 3 tablespoons cocoa
- 1 tablespoon grated lemon peel
- 1 tablespoon grated orange peel
- Grated coconut sprinkled & pressed on the icing

EVAPORATED MILK ICING
(Azucarado de Leche Evaporada)

1 cup Confectioners' sugar
1 cup evaporated milk
4 oz. butter
1 teaspoon vanilla
3 egg yolks

Mix all ingredients in top of double boiler, over medium heat and beat with electric mixer or hand beater for 12 to 15 minutes until mixture thickens to spreading consistency.

COCOA ICING
(Azucarado de Cocoa)

6 tablespoons butter – softened
Hershey's cocoa
- 1/3 cup for a light color
- ½ cup for a medium color
- ¾ cup for a dark color

2 2/3 cups Confectioner's sugar
1/3 cup milk
1 t teaspoon vanilla

Beat butter until creamy. Add cocoa and Confectioners' sugar, alternating with milk. Beat until creamy. Add vanilla and beat until the right consistency.

FLUFFY ICING
(Azucarado Esponjoso)

1/2 cup margarine
dash salt
4 cups Confectioner's sugar – sifted

3 tablespoons lemon juice
1 teaspoon grated lemon peel

Beat butter, salt and lemon juice. Add Confectioner's sugar slowly and beat until fluffy. Add grated lemon peel and continue beating until the desired consistency

MOCHA ICING
(Azucarado Moka)

1/2 cup margarine
1 2/3 cups sifted Confectioners' sugar
2 tablespoons cocoa

1/8 teaspoon salt
3 tablespoons strong hot coffee
1 teaspoon vanilla or rum

Beat all ingredients together until well mixed. Cool for 5 minutes, then beat until the desired consistency.

"NEVER FAIL" ICING
(Azucarado "Nunca Falla")

2 egg whites
1 1/2 cups sugar
5 tablespoons cold water

¼ teaspoon cream of tartar
1 ½ teaspoons white Karo syrup
1 teaspoon vanilla

Mix all ingredients in top of double boiler, over boiling water, beating constantly and slowly for 7 minutes with hand beater or electric mixer. Remove from lower part of double boiler and continue beating until of spreading consistency.

Lagniappe
(Something Extra)

Happy is he who has felt
the touch and warmth
of a friendly hand......

BUTTER ON THE WAR BEAT
(Mantequilla al Son de la Guerra)

½ lb. margarine or butter   ¾ cup evaporated milk
¼ teaspoon salt

Have margarine or butter at room temperature. Beat with salt until very creamy. Add milk slowly, beating continuously. When all the milk has been incorporated, beat for 1 more minute. Pour in mold. Keep refrigerated.

The start of World War II caused a nation-wide food rationing for mainland USA & territories. Ration books with stamps for each member of a family were issued and included instructions about the amount of meat, gasoline, sugar, and other essential products that a person was allowed to buy and would not be exceeded. Always resourceful, Puerto Ricans extended the amount of rationed butter or margarine with this recipe.

MINGA'S SOFRITO
(Sofrito "Mingo")

1/4 lb. sweet chiles   1 (8 oz.) can pimientos
1 lb. garlic cloves   1/2 lb. long leaf cilantro
1/4 lb. green leaf cilantro   1 cup fresh orégano or
1 lb. green peppers   2 tablespoons dry orégano

Grind in blender or meat grinder and mix well. Refrigerate or freeze.

TONY'S SEASONING A LA CREOLE
(Adobe Criollo "Tony")

1 box salt (1 lb. 10 ounces)   1 oz. garlic powder
1 1/2 oz. black pepper   1 oz. chili powder
2 oz. ground red pepper   1 oz. monosodium glutamate (Accent)

Mix all ingredients together and pack in glass jars. **For fish dishes add:**
  1 teaspoon thyme   1 teaspoon basil   1 teaspoon bay leaves (crushed)

LIME JUICE CONCENTRATE
(Jugo de Limón Concentrado)

1 cup lime juice
1 cup sugar
1/2 cup water

Mix ingredients together until sugar is dissolved. Freeze in plastic containers. To make lemonade add 3 parts water to 1 part concentrate.

You can freeze soursop (guanábana) juice, tropical cherry (acerola) juice and guava juice following the same instructions.

And for Last.......Tidbits.......
(Y por Último.......Consejitos.......)

1. You can use instant mashed potatoes in the following:
   a. Add 2 tablespoons dry instant mashed potatoes to 1 pound ground meat when making hamburgers or meat loaf.
   b. Add 1/2 tablespoon dry instant mashed potatoes for a two egg omelet.
   c. Use instant mashed potatoes as topping for casseroles or over stuffing, instead of Corn Flakes crumbs or beaten eggs. Use 1/2 cup instant mashed potatoes and 1 tablespoon melted butter.
2. Use nutmeg to enhance the flavor of boiled cabbage, spaghetti, meat balls, meat stews, pie crusts, creamed corn and corn niblets.
3. When boiling beans, add 1 teaspoon sugar to take away the acidity and to make the beans more flavorful.
4. When making egg cream or white sauce, if it gets lumpy, beat hard and the lumps will disappear, or use a wire whisk, egg beater or electric mixer.
5. When making Papaya in Syrup, after you peel and cube the papaya, soak it in water with 2 tablespoons baking powder or baking soda, to harden the slices on the outside so they will not get too mushy. Rinse, place in the pot, add the sugar, cover and simmer until cooked. If you would like more syrup, add more water and more sugar. After it boils and the sugar is dissolved, remove the lid and cook stirring occasionally until syrup is of the right consistency.
6. To obtain a nice golden syrup, caramelize some sugar in a skillet and stir slowly into the Papaya in Syrup and continue cooking candy until done.
7. To flavor meat stew, an onion stuck with several whole cloves will do the trick. Cook with the stew.
8. To thicken sauces, add cornstarch mixed with a small amount of water.
9. Guanábana refreshment is made with water... Guanábana Champola is made by adding milk. Wine may be added also.
10. Fruit peels can be frozen for later use. Store peeling of oranges, chironjas, grapefruits, lemons, lime and also guava shells in the freezer until ready to use or until you have enough to make candy or preserves.
11. Lemons are easily peeled with a vegetable peeler and lemon peels freeze very well for later use.

12. When ripe plantains are not ripe enough or soft enough for baking, you may "tenderize" them by rolling the unpeeled plantain on a board, or pound with a mallet until soft to the touch.
13. To save electric current, instead of using the oven, cook meat pies and casseroles on top of the stove. In this way you can make a yucca pie, yautía pie, ripe plantain casserole (piñón) and stuffed cabbage leaves.
14. When making stuffed cabbage leaves, instead of stuffing and rolling each leaf separately, make a cabbage pie. Layer the boiled cabbage leaves in a skillet, spoon the ground beef filling, sliced boiled eggs and top with another layer of cabbage leaves. Pour a mixture of tomato sauce and water over the pie, cover and simmer until done. You can line the skillet with a banana leaf and use another banana leaf on top for more flavor.
15. For your health, use margarine instead of butter.
16. Mangoes may be frozen. Mash mangoes and strain the pulp to be used for pies, mousse, ice cream, mango bread, cakes, or a delicious mango daiquiri. Freeze in covered plastic containers. Also freeze in slices that should be previously dipped in lime or lemon juice. Place one layer of mango slices on a tray and freeze, then store in plastic bags. Frozen mangoes can be eaten as is, or used in your favorite recipes.
17. Save left over boiled rice and add to cooked ground meat to use in stuffing for vegetables.

Alphabetical Index

Appetizers	**27**
Antipasto " Mamé"	30
Antipasto "Pepevé"	30
Borínquen Paté	35
Caribbean Caviar	35
Chicken Livers Mousse	35
Gizzards "Mamá Ina"	34
Latin Paté	36
Little Devils	36
Marinated Mushrooms	36
My Mother's Cocktail Onions	31
Old Time Foi Gras	32
Onion Quiche	32
Paté "Mamé"	33
Rainbow Sandwich	31
Tuna Mousse	32
Turkey Roll	32
Beverages and Short Drinks	**21**
Coffee Eggnog "Lía"	25
Delicious Hot Chocolate	24
Eggnog "Papai"	23
Irish Cream "Nenai"	24
Island Coconut Egg Nog	24
Kahlua "The Spiders"	23
Party Punch	26
Santa Rosa Sangría	25
Spiced Brew	23
Spiked Iced Tea	26
Breads	**129**
Banana Bread	134
Bread … Only Bread	165
Cinnamon Raisin Rolls "Carmela"	133
Coffee Ring	130
Corn Bread "Tía Delia"	134

Breads *(continued)*

Jalapeño Cornbread	132
Milkless Cornbread	134
Streusel Topping *(for Banana or any sweet bread)*	134
Sweet Potato and Coffee Bread	131
Sweet Potato Bread	131
Topping *(for Bread ... Only Bread)*	131
Walnut Bread	133

Cookies ... Cakes ... Icings ... 157

Apple Cake "Din"	161
Boiled Icing	172
Brown Cookies	164
Butter Icing	171
Caramel Icing	169
Chocolate Cookies	170
Christmas Cookies	165
Cocoa Icing	173
Coffee Cake and Nuts Cake	158
Cookies "Ana María"	166
Cookies "Leyla Rossy"	167
Cookies from Seville	167
Cowboy Cookies	166
Dainty Date Cookies	168
Date Fingers	167
Don Pedro's Marzipan Cake	160
Easy Chocolate Icing	171
Evaporated Milk Icing	172
Fluffy Icing	173
Glaze *(for Apple "Din" Cake)*	161
Glaze *(for Coffee Cake and Nuts)*	158
Hot Milk Cake "Mrs. Pelz"	163
Ice Box Cake "Carita"	163
Karo Icing *(and variations)*	172
Lace Cookies	160
"Mamá Celia's" Upside Down Cake	158
Mazapanes "Aurora"	166
Mocha Cake "Carmencita"	162
Mocha Icing *(for Mocha Cake "Carmencita")*	162

Cookies … Cakes … Icings … *(continued)*

Moist Cake "Carmen Luisa"	160
My Very Own Mazapanes	161
"Naná's" Cookies	169
"Never Fail" Icing	174
Orange Glaze	170
Refrigerator Cookies	169
Simply Cookies	169
Special Icing	171
White Cake with Sweet Wine	159
Sponge Cake	159
Sponge Cake "Lila"	165
Syrup *(for Mocha Cake "Carmencita", any cake)*	160
Syrup *(for Witch's Pound Cake)*	164
Witches Pound Cake	164

Desserts and Candies — **137**

Baked Puffs	143
Brandy Balls	146
Bread Pudding with Fruits	146
Breadfruit Pudding	145
Caramel	139,141,145,149,150,169
Caramel *(for The Big Meringue Waded)*	149
Caramel Icing	169
Chantilly "Didí"	155
Cheese Custard "Rina"	151
Coconut Cream "Livia I."	153
Coconut Custard	143
Coconut Custard "Luchi"	140
Coconut Delight	148
Cornmeal Mush with Coconut Milk	139
Cream of Rice "Yavita"	154
Don Julián's Lemon Pie	151
Egg Cream "doña Yuya"	150
Egg Custard	139
Filling *(for 2 Lemon Pies)*	151
Fudge "doña Asunción"	144
Grandma's Love Dust	149
Guava Jelly "Porta Coeli"	153

Desserts and Candies *(continued)*

Guava Shells Candy "Calle Luna"	147
Heavenly Bread Pudding	138
Imperial Cream "Guamá"	141
Mango Paste "Cotuí"	155
Marshmallow Syrup "Evan"	152
Marshmallow Syrup "Tía Mercedes"	152
Marzipan Apples "Zoé"	155
Maye's Meringues	155
Meringue *(for various desserts)*	138,141,148,149,151,155
Milk Fudge "Marianne"	144
Mother's Vol-au-Vent	143
Peach Custard "Mimi"	140
Pudding "Bono"	145
Pudding "Tía Bebé"	150
Pudding "Twin Bells"	148
Custard "Lillian"	142
Custard "Mamai"	142
Pumpkin Custard "San Martín"	144
Rum Balls	154
San Germán Floating Island	153
Sweet Potato Candy	156
Sweet Rice Coconut "Beba"	138
Syrup *(for Baked Puffs)*	140
Syrup *(for Vol-Au-Vent & any dessert)*	141
Tastes So Good "Mamachita"	145
The Big Meringue "Waded"	149
The Islands *(for San Germán Floating Islands)*	154
"Tío Pepe's" Bread Pudding	147
To Make Coconut Milk	152
White Fudge "Divinity"	156

Egg Dishes — 55

Asparagus Soufflé	58
Caribbean Omelet	57
Cheese Soufflé	59
Egg in Jacket	56
Egg Stuffed Potatoes	56
Eggs Malagueña	59
Green Pea Omelet	59

Egg Dishes *(continued)*

Ham Omelet	59
Omelet for Lent	57
Spaghetti Omelet	568
Sweet Omelet	56
White Sauce *(for Eggs in Jacket)*	56

Fish and Seafood — 83

Baked Fish Jardinière "Araceli"	89
Bonito Roll	84
Codfish Pudding	89
Codfish Stomach "Mina"	85
Cold Salmon	86
Filling *(for Tuna Pie "Guaro")*	86
Fish Pudding "Irma"	88
Fish Pudding "Tío Pepe"	87
Petit Aioli *(for Codfish and Vegetables or other fish)*	86
Petit Aioli with Codfish and Vegetables	85
Salmon Soufflé	87
Shrimp Creole	84
Shrimp in Garlic Sauce	84
Shrimp Scampi	84
Tartar Sauce *(for any fish)*	87
Tuna Fish or Salmon Pudding with Cornflakes	90
Tuna Pie "Guaro"	88

Fritters — 113

Corn Meal Fritters	115
Corn Meal Sticks with Coconut	116
Creamed Corn Fritters	117
Doughnuts "Poly"	116
Garbanzo Fritters	117
Grains of Rice from the east	115
"Mamá Celia's" Doughnuts	118
Ñame Fritters "Lelé"	117
Old Woman's Bellies "Minillas"	116
Rice Meal Fritters "doña Ana"	114
Rice Meal Fritters "Isabel"	114

Fritters (continued)
San Germán Codfish Fritters	115
Yautía Fritters	114

Meats — **61**

About Pork Offal	66
Baked Ham	68
Batter *(for Stuffed Pimentos Salazar)*	73
Beef "Inesita"	63
Beef "María"	63
Beef Cutlets	65
Beef Steak "a la Lola"	64
Beef Steak with Green Peppers	62
Breaded Pig's Feet	68
Breading Ingredients *(for Pig's Feet or any meats)*	68
Cabbage Pie "Marina"	72
"Carol's" Pork Chops	66
Cold Eye of Round Roast	69
Cold Roast Beef in "Deer" Marinade	74
"Deer" Marinade *(for Beef or Pork)*	74
Dough *(for Yuca turnovers)*	67
Filling *(for Yuca Turnovers)*	67
Filling *(for Stuffed Leg of Pork)*	75
Ham Loaf	72
Kid or Goat "Paca"	65
Lyonnaise Sausage "Mami"	74
Meat Balls "doña Virginia"	62
Our Very Own Stuffed Cheese	71
Pork Meat Roll	70
Pork Offal	67
Ragged Meat Stew	65
Roast beef "Olga and Celia"	73
Sauce for the Meat *(for Cold Eye of Round)*	69
Savory Meat Loaf	69
To Make Simple Sofrito	71
Steak and Beer	75
Stewed Cured Meat	65
Stuffed Leg of Pork "Tía Bebé"	72
Stuffed Pimentos "Salazar"	73
Sweet and Sour Pork "doña Juana"	65
Yuca Turnovers	67

Pastas	99
Bechamel Sauce *(for Chicken Lasagna)*	106
"Carol's" Spaghetti Sauce	106
Chicken Lasagna	103
Filling *(for Lasagna with Bacon and Chicken)*	102
Green Pasta	101
Lasagna with Bacon and Chicken	102
Macaroni Soufflé	105
Macaroni Stuffed Peppers	104
Macaroni Timbale	106
Neapolitan Fettuccini	100
Noodles "San José"	101
Pasta Primavera "Lelé"	110
Ring of Plenty	100
Roman Pasta	100
Spaghetti Carbonara "July"	106
Spaghetti Sauce	103
White Sauce *(for Lasagna with Bacon and Chicken)*	102
Poultry	77
Basting Ingredients *(for Stuffed Turkey)*	80
Breading *(for Chicken Surprises)*	82
Chicken "à la Julie"	81
Chicken "Porta Coeli"	79
Chicken Breast "Rebeca"	81
Chicken in Onion and Egg Sauce "Tía Rita"	82
Chicken Stuffed with "Mofongo"	79
Chicken Stuffed with Vegetables	81
Chicken Surprises	82
Guinea Hen in Chocolate Gravy "Mamá Chita)	78
Mofongo *(for Chicken Stuffed with "Mofongo")*	79
Sauce *(for Chicken à la "Julie")*	80
Stuffed Chicken Legs	78
Stuffed Turkey	80
Stuffing *(for Chicken Legs)*	78
Poultry *(continued)*	
Stuffing *(for Stuffed Turkey)*	80

Rice and Grains	**117**
Baked Rice with Pork Chops	125
Beans in Salsa Moo	123
Black Beans	124
Chicken and Rice with Beer	118
Fried Garbanzos "Mamá"	126
Fried Navy Beans	118
Garbanzo Casserole "Irma"	121
Good Friday Rice	126
Lima Beans with Spanish Sausage	120
Navy Beans with Codfish "a la Yaurel"	125
Pickled Pigeon Peas "Quique"	124
Rice "Alhambra"	120
Rice "Santa Rosa"	123
Rice and Pickled Fish "San Luis"	119
Rice Ring	119
Rice with Asparagus	119
Rice with Cabbage	120
Rice with Okra	122
Rice with Vienna Sausages and Red Wine	122
Sauce *(for Garbanzo Casserole Irma)*	21
Stuffed Rice	121
Salads	**47**
Crazy Chicken Salad	49
Florida Salad	48
Glaze for Potato Salad	53
Macaroni and Shrimp Salad	48
Morsel from the sea	52
Pear Salad	49
Potato and Chicken Salad	53
Potato Roll	49
Rainbow Salad "Yuya"	51
Salad Boat	52
Spring Salad	50
Stuffed Tomatoes	51

Sauces	**107**
Ajilimójili	108
White Sauce	100
Aioli or Garlic Sauce	108
Anchovy Vinaigrette	111
Avocado dressing or Guacamole	108
Bechamel Sauce	110
Bechamel Sauce with Egg	110
Butter Sauce	109
Garlic Mayonnaise	109
Maître D'hôtel Sauce	111
Sauce for Vegetables	111
Vinaigrette Sauce *(for Lobster or Fish)*	109
Soups and Stews	**39**
Bollitos	40
Catalonian Soup	45
Chili	43
Codfish Asopao	40
Galician Soup	41
Garbanzo Purée	42
Garbanzo Soup with Chicken	43
Garlic and Onion Soup	41
Garlic Soup	40
"Mofongo" and Egg Soup	44
Pigeon Pea *(Gandules)* Stew	42
Soup for Lent	44
The Catalonian Meatball *(for Catalonian Soup)*	45
Lagniappe *(Something Extra)*	**175**
And for Last … Tidbits …	178
Butter on the War Beat	178
Lime Juice Concentrate	176
"Minga's" Sofrito	176
Tony's Seasoning "a la Creole"	176
Vegetables	**91**
Baked Eggplant with Cheese	92
Baked Pumpkin	98
Corn and Carrots Soufflé	97
Corn Soufflé "Mimí"	97

Vegetables *(continued)*

Country Eggplant	93
Country Style Yautía "Berty"	93
Duchess Potatoes	96
Eggplant Au Gratin	94
Garlic Potatoes	95
Glazed Carrots	92
Glazed Sweet Potatoes	93
Potato and Bacon Pie	96
Scrambled Mirlitons	92
Sweet and Sour Beets	94
Sweet and Sour String Beans	64
Sweet Green Peas with Ham and Red Wine	97
Vegetable Soufflé	95
Vegetables à la Grecque "Fragoso"	95

www.ingramcontent.com/pod-product-compliance
Lightning Source LLC
Chambersburg PA
CBHW080734230426
43665CB00020B/2729